D1559269

THE CHRIST CHILD ——
GOES TO COURT

THE CHRIST CHILD GOES TO COURT

Wayne R. Swanson

TEMPLE UNIVERSITY PRESS
Philadelphia

Temple University Press, Philadelphia 19122
Copyright © 1990 by Temple University. All rights reserved
Published 1990
Printed in the United States of America

The paper used in this publication meets the minimum
requirements of American National Standard for Information Sciences—Permanence of Paper for Printed Library
Materials, ANSI Z39.48-1984 ∞

LIBRARY OF CONGRESS CATALOGING-IN-PUBLICATION DATA

Swanson, Wayne R.
    The Christ child goes to court.
    Bibliography: p.
    Includes index.
    1. Donnelly, Daniel—Trials, litigation, etc.
2. Lynch, Dennis M.—Trials, litigation, etc.
3. Ecclesiastical Law—Rhode Island—Pawtucket.
4. Creches (Nativity scenes)—Rhode Island—Pawtucket.
I. Title.
KF228.D66S93   1990   342.73'0852   89-4654
                            347.302852
ISBN 0-87722-638-5

To my parents

CONTENTS

PREFACE

THIS BOOK HAS TWO MAJOR PURPOSES. The first objective is to add to the limited number of case studies that are available as textbooks for courses in American politics. During twenty years of college teaching I have listened to colleagues lament that the discipline suffers from a lack of good case studies. *The Christ Child Goes to Court* was written in response to this perceived gap in political science literature. It is my hope that those who read about the controversy surrounding Pawtucket, Rhode Island's efforts to display the Christmas Nativity scene will be better informed about the process by which the judiciary functions in the United States, and the role of the federal courts in the political system.

The second purpose of this book is to analyze one of the most difficult problems posed by the First Amendment, the attempt to define and delineate the proper relationship between church and state. With the possible exception of the period during which the country was founded, at no other time in our history has the relationship between government and religion occupied a more important position on our political agenda. Although the issue is hotly debated throughout the land and in all of our halls of government, the courts have had and will continue to have a special role in determining what the First Amendment means when it states that government "shall make no law respecting the establishment of religion." *Lynch v. Donnelly* is an especially good case to illustrate the difficulties that the issue poses not only for the courts, but also for the political system as a whole.

While I have attempted to present a balanced view of a subject that is extremely controversial, the reader will have little difficulty discerning my preference for a strict separationist view of church–state questions. The major reason for spelling out my own opinion is not simply to persuade readers that my analysis is correct, but also to stimulate readers on all sides of the question to pursue this important First Amendment issue beyond the material presented here. This is a complicated political question with no quick or easy answers.

I am indebted to Professor Martha Joynt Kumar of Towson State College for encouraging me to move ahead on the project. The fascination of my students at Connecticut College for the constitutional dilemma that the Nativity scene thrust on the courts convinced me that the issue was an unusually compelling one.

Special thanks go to Professor Caren Dubnoff of Holy Cross College, who was a source of intellectual stimulation on church–state questions during an Institute for European Studies seminar in England during the summer of 1987. Her perceptive critique of the manuscript made a significant contribution to the organization of the book.

C. Herman Pritchett, the author of the assigned text in my first course in constitutional law, also reviewed the manuscript. My debt to him is not only for his helpful comments on the manuscript, but for the contributions he has made to the study of constitutional law throughout his career.

Connecticut College has been generous in providing the time and financial resources to make the book possible. Dean Harold Juli, associate dean of the faculty, was especially helpful. Cathy Smith provided valuable typing skills while I was mastering the Macintosh Plus. Elina Sharp was always available to lend a helping hand. Close friends like Joan King cheerfully tolerated the moods of exhilaration and frustration that all authors experience. Although they do not bear any specific responsibility for the pages which follow, it is because of stimulating role models like Professors George Goodwin, Jr., of the University of Massachusetts in Boston, Elmer E. Cornwell, Jr., of Brown University, and David D. Warren of the University of Rhode Island that I was able to write the book.

For the opportunities they provided, their moral support, patience, understanding, and countless other qualities, this book is dedicated to my parents.

THE CHRIST CHILD
GOES TO COURT

INTRODUCTION

Scarcely any political question arises in the United States that
is not resolved, sooner or later, into a judicial question.

Alexis de Tocqueville, *Democracy in America*

THE JUDICIARY IN THE UNITED STATES performs an indis-
pensable role in resolving the nation's most difficult problems. History clearly shows that the major questions that claim a
position on our political agenda invariably make it to the courts'
dockets. This has been especially true during the last half-
century, when an era of "big government" spawned by Franklin
Roosevelt's New Deal raised the stakes in American politics.
Conflicts over who should benefit from government's increasing
generosity invited disputes that go to the heart of the Constitution. As questions relating to the appropriate balance between
majority rule and minority rights became involved in the struggles
for political power and favor, the judicial branch of government
was asked to provide many of the most important answers. Government policies relating to segregation, sex discrimination,
criminal due process, political, social, and economic equality, and
freedom of religion are conspicuous among the landmark judicial decisions of the period.

Because it is positioned at the highest point in the judicial
hierarchy, the Supreme Court is the final arbiter of constitutional struggles. The Court's paramount importance in the areas
of civil liberties and individual rights is explained in part by its

3

willingness to confront issues that the elected branches of government and the lower courts have been unwilling or unable to handle. Life tenure provides the justices with an insulated position from which to make the "tough" decisions that their politically vulnerable colleagues in government often choose to avoid. Although the public does not automatically embrace its rulings, few Americans would dispute the fact that the Court is the final authority about the meaning of the Constitution.

In some instances the issues that secure a place on the judicial agenda gradually disappear. Court rulings often provide the guidelines that help to solve problems. Many conflicts persist, however. The courts are not always able to devise judicial standards to settle constitutional disputes. Sometimes the failure lies with the political complexity of the controversy. Even the judiciary is not totally immune from the pressures of "ordinary" politics. In other instances the problem is with the peculiar mix of attitudes of the judges. Difficult constitutional issues are quick to bring out the ideological divisions that exist on the bench. More often a combination of both factors impinges on the process when a difficult case is being argued.

A troublesome issue for American politics is separation of church and state. Experience taught our founders that religion can be a powerful motivating force that often leads its proponents to enlist the power of the state to propagate their beliefs. History has also taught us that societies which fail to depoliticize religion often generate internally explosive divisions that are potentially self-destructive.

For these reasons the Framers of the Bill of Rights put freedom of religion in a prominent position. The First Amendment begins by stipulating that "Congress shall make no law respecting the establishment of religion, nor prohibiting the free exercise thereof." Questions over what constitutes an "establishment" of religion and when the government's interest may prevail

over claims of "free exercise" of religion have become more frequent in the era of the welfare state. How much cooperation can
exist between church and state without constituting an "establishment" of religion? How much nonconformity must be tolerated to preserve the "free exercise" of religion?

In December 1980, the Rhode Island affiliate of the American Civil Liberties Union (ACLU) challenged the constitutionality of the city of Pawtucket's use of taxpayer money to erect and
display the Christmas Nativity scene. Because opponents of the
practice saw the city's display of the manger as an endorsement
of Christianity, the practice was alleged to violate the Establishment Clause of the First Amendment.

When matters of faith become a source of public controversy, the emotional conflicts that are produced put a major
strain on politics. The ACLU suit precipitated a spirited debate
in Rhode Island that raised the divergent traditions, beliefs, and
ways of life of its citizens to a prominent place on the political
agenda. No matter how familiar the Nativity scene may seem or
how small the amount of money involved, the dispute was not
trivial. It raised a significant constitutional question over the extent to which the religious majority could use the machinery of
government to celebrate and spread its teachings.

This book follows the Nativity scene case as it wound its
way through three levels in the federal court system. Thirty-nine
months elapsed between the time that the suit was initiated by
the ACLU and the decision of the Supreme Court in *Lynch v.
Donnelly* on 5 March 1984.

The judiciary is the least known and understood of the three
branches of our national government. One objective of this
study is to educate about the judicial process and the role that
the courts, particularly the Supreme Court, play in the political
system. A second goal is to discuss the arguments that form the
basis of the dispute over the meaning of "separation of church

and state." Hopefully, the book will stimulate the reader to explore even further a constitutional question that judges and citizens find most perplexing.

Case studies are valuable in political science because they provide concrete illustrations of the political system at work. They manifest the "struggle among groups for power," the "authoritative allocation of values," "conflict resolution" processes, and the "art of compromise," which is what politics is all about. More than other methods, case studies bring to light the inevitable connections in politics between the wide-ranging priorities of the individuals who make up the system and the institutions created to respond to their divergent needs. They also provide a more realistic picture of political performance. Lest we be lulled into the fairy tale promise that "they all lived happily thereafter," the end result of a political controversy often leads to an imperfect solution. Politics is an essential and inevitable activity, but it may not hold all of the answers to society's problems.

The idea for *The Christ Child Goes to Court* grew out of a strong conviction that the Nativity scene case was an excellent example to illustrate the workings of the judicial process in the United States and to show how the courts' interpretation of the Constitution helps to shape the development of public policy. Too often textbooks in American politics are limited to a broad overview of the judiciary. An incomplete picture of the way in which the judiciary functions and its impact on the larger political system often results. By masking much of the complexity and behind-the-scenes activity of the courts, the standard fare oversimplifies and often understates the judiciary's role.

The Nativity scene controversy is an unusually captivating topic. First, it raises a compelling constitutional issue to which all readers can relate. Christians, members of other religious denominations, or persons with no religious preference are quick to take sides on the question. Second, the lines of arguments and emotional intensity of the debate cause most people to question their first reaction to the issue. The political process has a way of complicating questions that first appear to be easily resolved. Finally, no matter whether one agrees or disagrees with the courts' resolution of the issue, the end result is disappointing. The reality is that although a case was decided, the issue of government sponsorship of Nativity scenes and other religious symbols is still alive.

Considerations of process are not the only factor that makes *Lynch v. Donnelly* an attractive case study. Since the mid-1940s, when they began to appear with some regularity on the dockets, substantive issues of separation of church and state have presented the judiciary with its most burdensome First Amendment problems. The language employed in the religion clauses asks the courts to develop a standard to maintain the delicate balance between individuals' right to freely practice their religious beliefs and the need to guard against church–state relationships that would promote the establishment of religion.

The challenge has been formidable. The Supreme Court's efforts have produced a series of "hopelessly divided" judgments, which many judges and constitutional scholars acknowledge have shed less light than confusion on the issue. The failure to agree on an acceptable interpretation of establishment has perpetuated and intensified religious conflicts in American politics. By weighing the courts' decisions in *Lynch v. Donnelly* in the context of church–state rulings that preceded and followed it, we are able to trace the historical evolution of an important and timely issue in American constitutional law.

Finally, the methods employed by judges to reach their decisions about government-sponsored Nativity scenes and other church–state controversies raise a more fundamental question about the role of the courts in American politics. A scholarly dispute about the scope of judicial power calls attention to two competing theories. On the one side of the debate are those persons who believe that constitutional law must be derived from values found or implied in the text of the Constitution, from the intentions of the Founding Fathers, or in the "historical understandings" of the Constitution. In the opposing camp are the individuals who argue that because it is difficult to apply the words of the Framers to contemporary problems, judges must look to evolving political conditions that often transcend the original history surrounding the Constitution's adoption.

The Reagan administration, through its judicial appointments and in the speeches of Attorney General Edwin Meese and other officials, has vigorously attacked "activist" judges bent more on "legislating public policy" than "interpreting" constitutional text. Supreme Court justice William J. Brennan, the target of much of the criticism, has become a major spokesman for the expansive view of the judicial role. Because the intention of the Framers and the historical place of religion in American history were significant factors in the Nativity scene debate, the courts' decisions can be said to have turned at least in part on matters affecting the question of judicial role.

A good case study performs six major tasks. These serve as criteria for the organization of this book. First, the conditions that brought the parties into court are discussed. What is the constitutional issue, who were the litigants, and what was the nature of the political and social setting in which the case was argued? Second, the relationship of the case to prior court decisions is documented. Because few, if any, cases raise issues that are unique to the judicial agenda, it is important to understand the "legal context" in which the case was decided. Third, the movement of the case within the judicial system is described. In general, how do cases move from one court to another, and what conditions must exist for a litigant to appeal a lower court decision successfully? Fourth, the decisions of the three courts are analyzed. What were the reasons for the decisions, and what standards did the courts use to decide the case? Wherever appropriate, the text relies on the written briefs, petitions, court opinions, and other documents connected with the suit.

Just as the judiciary does not attend to a constitutional issue without prior court activity, neither does the judicial process end with a Supreme Court decision. Chapter V reports the reaction of the general public to the ruling. The responses of the media, interest groups, legal scholars, and average citizens determine the degree to which a decision settles a constitutional dispute. No court decision is so final that it precludes other attempts to reexamine an issue. A sixth task is to look at subsequent judicial decisions. Do they strengthen or modify the Nativity scene ruling? Although a single dispute becomes the focus of analysis, a good case study will provide a broader perspective that draws attention to the evolutionary process that shapes the manner by which the judiciary interprets the Constitution.

The book concludes with the author's assessment of the decision and its impact on the First Amendment's provision relating to separation of church and state. Was the decision correct? Was the Supreme Court's approach to establishment law sound? In what other directions might the Court have moved? On an issue that generates such a divergence of opinion, the ultimate objective of the text is not so much to answer questions as it is to raise them. The goal is also to leave sufficient room for readers to come to their own resolution of the problem.

THE ACLU AND PAWTUCKET'S CHRISTMAS DISPLAY: The Controversy Unfolds

I am sorry that the Mayor doesn't recognize the constitutional obligation he is under to uphold the First Amendment. The principle of separation of church and state is a very important one and a Nativity Scene display sponsored and paid for by the City can be extremely offensive to members of other faiths. The Mayor and other city officials simply have no business getting involved in religious activity.

Stephen Brown, executive director of the
Rhode Island chapter of the ACLU

Every Christmas needs a Scrooge and the ACLU is the Scrooge this year.

Pawtucket mayor Dennis M. Lynch

T HE UNITED STATES HAD KNOWN better times than December 1980. Anxieties ran high. The holiday spirit was not all bright lights and tinsel. The economy was out of control. Numbers told the story. Unemployment, interest rates, and inflation were all in double digits. OPEC had become a symbol of anger and frustration as gasoline and heating oil costs soared over a dollar a gallon. Daily reminders by the media that fifty-three American hostages in Iran were in their fourteenth month of captivity had an hypnotizing and psychologically draining effect. Jimmy Carter was about to vacate the White House. Ronald Reagan was waiting in the wings. Gallup reported that Pope John Paul II was America's most admired leader.

In Pawtucket, Rhode Island, the city's colorful Christmas display belied the real holiday mood. A mixture of fear and apprehension about the rising costs of food, fuel, and housing, not to mention Christmas gifts, gripped the city. One resident complained, "There's just no way out of the vicious circle they're putting people into. It keeps getting worse and worse. It wipes the Christmas spirit right out."[1] As if national political and economic woes were not enough to dampen the holiday season, Pawtucket became the hotbed of its own controversy in 1980. At the center of the conflict was a city-owned Nativity scene.

On 17 December 1980, just eight days before Christmas, the Rhode Island affiliate of the ACLU took Pawtucket to court. The suit, filed in the U.S. district court in Providence, alleged that the manger scene in the city's Christmas display was a violation of the First Amendment's provisions relating to separation of church and state. (Because the suit concerned a potential violation of the national Constitution, the case was tried in a federal rather than a state court.) Specifically the ACLU complained that Pawtucket's use of taxpayers' money to support a religious display that depicted the biblical description of the birth of Christ amounted to government promotion of religion, a practice, they argued, that clearly contravened the Establishment Clause of the First Amendment.

The lawsuit was brought on behalf of Daniel Donnelly, a Pawtucket resident and ACLU member. Donnelly agreed to become coplaintiff at the request of Stephen Brown, the executive director of the Rhode Island ACLU. Brown sought Donnelly's support after he received an anonymous phone call from a Pawtucket woman who objected to the Nativity scene. Named as defendants were Pawtucket's mayor, Dennis M. Lynch, the city finance director, Richard A. Mumford, and the parks and recreation director, Guy Dufault. The ACLU asked the court to issue a temporary restraining order, which would require the immediate removal of the manger scene from the display.

Two days after the suit was filed, Raymond J. Pettine, chief judge of the federal district court, postponed a ruling on the request for the restraining order. The judge stated that the Pawtucket dispute raised serious and delicate questions of constitutional law, which deserved more thorough consideration than he could give if pressed for an immediate decision. Pettine also noted that the suit came "less than a week before Christmas, at a time when emotions run high and the response to a case of this type is likely to be grounded in passion rather than reason."[2] A fact-finding trial was scheduled for early in the new year.

The constitutional issue raised by *Donnelly v. Lynch* is not a simple one. (At this point in the case Donnelly's name is listed first because he is the petitioner. Mayor Lynch is the defendant. When the case reaches the Supreme Court, the names and roles are reversed [see page 109].) The First Amendment states in part that "Congress shall make no law respecting the establishment of religion, or prohibiting the free exercise thereof." Two constitutional protections are included in the religion clauses. "Free exercise of religion," not the central issue in Pawtucket, is the easier to interpret. The freedom to believe and practice one's beliefs has been broadly protected by the courts, particularly since *Sherbert v. Verner* (1963), which held that only a compelling state interest could justify limitation on religious liberties. Barring the rare instance when an individual's freedom to exercise religious beliefs comes into conflict with society's need for order and tranquility (e.g., the practice of polygamy, or the refusal to submit to smallpox vaccinations), the courts have most often championed freedom of religion, even when specific beliefs and practices are obnoxious to the vast majority of Americans.[3]

But what of the phrase, "respecting the establishment" of religion? Does Pawtucket "establish" religion by displaying the Nativity scene? Did the Constitution's Framers mean the Establishment Clause to eliminate all religious symbolism from government-sponsored activities? Is there a line that can be drawn between the ACLU position that any and all support of religion by government is a violation of the First Amendment and the position of others that, given religion's central place in American history and culture, some government acknowledgment and recognition of the nation's spiritual heritage is not only constitutional, but eminently desirable?

The courts have found it enormously difficult to proscribe workable guidelines to decide Establishment Clause cases. Former chief justice Warren E. Burger has written that "we can only dimly perceive the lines of demarcation in this extraordinarily sensitive area of constitutional law."[4] Another observer has characterized the Supreme Court's approach to establishment as "zigzagging its way through a minefield of competing and passionate viewpoints."[5]

Donnelly v. Lynch came at a time when the national mood was in great flux. The involvement of religious groups in politics was growing. Television ministries like Jerry Falwell's Moral Majority and Jim Bakker's PTL were reaching millions of Americans with an attack on the government's liberal social policies. Ronald Reagan had just been elected with the support of a religious constituency that had long been critical of the courts' positions on establishment. The issue of abortion divided the country. The shifting alignment of Roman Catholics and Evangelical Protestants toward the conservative views of the Republican party tended to polarize attitudes on social issues, many of which had strong religious roots. Those who worried that the growing political power of the "Religious Right" might undercut the po-

litical pragmatism and spirit of tolerance in our socially pluralistic nation wondered just how the courts' view of the First
Amendment would mesh with the new swing toward religious
fundamentalism.

Pawtucket was not the first community to become embroiled
in controversy over the observance of Christmas. After languish-
ing in court for almost five years, the Rhode Island ACLU
dropped its case against Providence, when the city stopped displaying the manger scene on City Hall steps. In Denver, Colorado, the federal district court permitted the city to display its
Nativity scene.[6] In early 1980, the courts turned down the pleas
of an atheist family in Sioux Falls, South Dakota, who objected
to the singing of "Silent Night" in their son's public school
Christmas program. The U.S. Circuit Court of Appeals in St.
Louis ruled that the practice was primarily educational, fostering "the advancement of the students' knowledge of society's
cultural and religious beliefs."[7]

Other communities have resolved Christmas disputes without going to court. Acting on complaints from Jewish leaders,
the town of Larchmont, New York, removed a Nativity scene
from Town Hall in 1975. A plan by which the creche rotates annually among three local churches was established. The town's
clergy issued a statement which said that "the creche is not a
universal but a sectarian, particularistic symbol. Its appropriate
place is not on tax supported property, but in our churches or on
their properties and in our homes."[8]

The Wake County, North Carolina, school board decided in
1977 to replace Christmas parties with an educational unit designed to encourage a broad recognition of the meaning of the
holiday season, rather than a narrow view restricted to Christmas. A year later the San Antonio, Texas, Council of Churches,
in an effort to avoid discrimination against non-Christian children, requested that the religious aspects of Christmas not be
observed in the city's public schools.

Minority religious groups, often reluctant to disrupt their communities by raising constitutional claims, have found other ways to sensitize public officials. In a pamphlet entitled "The December Dilemma," the American Jewish Committee alerted school officials to the uncomfortable predicament faced at Christmastime by children who are not Christian. "If they join in celebration and song about religious figures they do not acknowledge, they feel disloyal to their families and their traditions. If they refrain, they are made to feel like outsiders."[9]

Does the "seasonal identity crisis" of minority religious groups and nonbelievers raise legitimate Establishment Clause questions? Where does Pawtucket's Nativity scene place on the scales of justice? From a religious perspective, keeping Christ in Christmas is a commendable activity for Christians. But does government overstep the limits of the First Amendment when it joins in that effort?

PAWTUCKET REACTS

Pawtucket, Rhode Island, is an aging mill town situated on the Blackstone River four miles northeast of Providence. Its name derives from the Indian, meaning "the place by the waterfall." The city is located on land purchased from the Narragansett Indians in 1638 by Roger Williams, the colonial champion of religious liberty. Williams and his Baptist followers founded Rhode Island as a religious refuge from Massachusetts' Puritan-dominated government. The fourth largest city in Rhode Island, with a predominantly working-class population of seventy-one thousand, Pawtucket is one of the most ethnically diverse towns in the state. French, Irish, Italian, Portuguese, Polish, and Hispanic communities are spread throughout the city's nine square miles. Over 70 percent of the residents are Roman Catholic.

David R. Carlin, Jr., a Rhode Island state senator and sociologist at the University of Rhode Island, who grew up in Pawtucket, understands the city and its people. His perspectives help to explain the setting for the controversy.

Pawtucket is one of those places it's hard to love unless you were born and brought up there. It is a working-class and lower-middle-class town, with the former more numerous than the latter. It's doubtful that there is even a single person . . . who can claim upper-class status. It has occasional millionaires, to be sure, but their lifestyle is of middle-class or even working-class inspiration.

Though of course I didn't realize it at the time, Pawtucket was a kind of protective ghetto when I was growing up. It kept us oblivious to the not very flattering judgments the world at large was inclined to make on people like us. In the pre-Kennedy, pre–Vatican II era, Catholics were still regarded with some suspicion and disdain by their fellow citizens. But in Pawtucket we had no sense of this, no feeling of inferiority. Being Catholic, it seemed was the most normal thing in the world.

And in the age of rapid middle-class-ification and suburbanization that followed World War II, the working class . . . fell into increasing disesteem, while working-class cities like Pawtucket were held by the upwardly mobile in positive contempt. But we knew little or nothing of this.

Since those days Catholics have entered the mainstream of American life and don't need protective ghettos anymore. But the working class still needs shelter, needs it more than ever perhaps, in a society which in the last few decades has made it increasingly difficult, both financially and culturally, for workers and their families to be full-fledged participants in the national life. Without that shelter, alienation, resentment, and disorientation flourish. Pawtucket is still a city that does an effective job of providing that shelter.[10]

In the 1790s, when Samuel Slater built the first successful cotton mill operated by water power, Pawtucket became a major textile manufacturing center. It was once the thread-making capital of the world. Although the textile industry deserted New England for the South more than two generations ago, Slater's Mill has been restored as a textile and waterpower technology museum and is today a national historical site.

Pawtucket's economy is still struggling to recover from the loss of its major industrial base. Small manufacturers of plastics, chemicals, electronic equipment, jewelry, toys, and other assorted businesses dot the downtown area. Urban redevelopment has provided improved housing, and downtown shopping has been stimulated by APEX and Peerless, two major retail outlets that share the inner city with City Hall and the Slater Museum. Because the Christmas season is vital to the retail economy, city officials and retail merchants actively promote the city's holiday display, which annually brings large numbers of shoppers into the downtown area. David Carlin observes that "suburban malls and shopping centers . . . devastated Pawtucket's once

> flourishing business district. In those days downtown merchants didn't need the help of the baby Jesus to draw plentiful supplies of Christmas shoppers. To one who remembers Pawtucket in its heydey, the business district today feels like a ghost town. It seems harsh that constitutional scruples should deprive the few remaining downtown merchants of the little ghostly aid available to them.[11]

The city has sponsored a Christmas display for as long as most residents can remember. For many years it was located in Slater Park on the outskirts of town. In 1973, when vandalism became a serious problem in the park and the downtown area was being economically revitalized, Mayor Lynch moved the display to Hodgson Park on the banks of the Blackstone River adjacent to City Hall. The park consists of approximately forty thousand square feet and is privately owned by the Slater Museum Trust. The city's two largest retail establishments are within walking distance. Mayor Lynch and the museum director entered into an oral agreement that permits the city to use the park each holiday season. The city owns the Nativity scene, which it purchased in 1973 for $1,375. Municipal employees plan and erect the display. The city reimburses the museum for electricity costs.

Although it occupies a relatively small portion of the total display, the Nativity scene is located at the forefront. The figures in the scene, which are approximately life-sized, include kings bearing gifts, shepherds, animals, angels, Mary, Joseph, and the Christ Child. Several of the figures have their hands folded and are kneeling, conveying an atmosphere of devotion and worship.

The remainder of the display consists of other Christmas symbols. A Santa house is often inhabited by a live Santa Claus who distributes candy to children. A group of reindeer pulling Santa's sleigh is set on an elevated runway. There is a small village composed of four houses and a church surrounded by carolers in old-fashioned dress. A live forty-foot Christmas tree strung with lights, a talking wishing well, a long garland hung from candy-striped poles, and twenty-one cutout figures representing such characters as a clown, a dancing elephant, a robot, and a teddy bear are also part of the display. A large sign colored in fluorescent paint that spells "Seasons Greetings" welcomes visitors to the park. Carlin remembers the display fondly. "It created that air of sentimental solemnity, which is perfect for a child's Christmas. I have no doubt it contributed to both my religious formation and to my affection for Pawtucket—an affection which abides even though I left the city a dozen years ago." [12]

The timing of the suit brought a swift and passionate response from the public. The reaction was almost universal outrage that the ACLU would challenge this longstanding community tradition. The day after he was sued, Mayor Lynch staged an emotional rally and press conference in front of the Nativity scene, where he denounced the action as "a petty attack aimed at taking Christ out of Christmas." ACLU spokesman Stephen Brown publicly condemned the mayor's media event as an example of the kind of divisiveness that is generated when religion is used for political purposes. Not only did publicity from the suit arouse the feelings of the citizens of Pawtucket and Rhode Island, but national media and press coverage sparked letters and phone calls to the mayor's office from all over the country.

Press, radio, and television had a field day with the story. The Nativity scene dominated local radio talk shows. Callers bombarded the airwaves with praise for Mayor Lynch and disdain for the ACLU. Steve Kass, WHJJ talkmaster, reported, "In terms of steady constant comment, I can't think of anything else that has outraged more people. People said they dialed for hours and couldn't get through." [13] A *Pawtucket Times* editorial was supportive of the city.

> The ACLU suit against the City of Pawtucket is absurd. The problem here, surely, is not that the City is promoting religion with taxpayers' money. The problem is that a group like the ACLU, set up to defend the liberties of all of us, has apparently found itself with so few important battles to fight that it has time, money, and energy to squander on this absurd nitpicking at a season tradition that brings pleasure to us all. [14]

Over 90 percent of the mail and phone calls that came to the Pawtucket municipal offices and to the ACLU was on the side of the city. Donnelly, ACLU coplaintiff, was shunned and verbally attacked by individuals who recognized him from television and newspaper photographs.

> I knew the suit would not make me the most popular person in Rhode Island. But I wasn't prepared for the intensity of the reaction. Co-workers gave me the cold shoulder. People just assumed that I was an atheist or anti-Christ. They didn't even want to hear what I had to say.

I am a Roman Catholic and I felt torn about objecting to anything that was tied so closely to my background. But I didn't feel comfortable with public depictions of spirituality. I've been concerned that various religious groups are becoming more and more political and are trying to impose their views on the larger society. To me the Nativity Scene represented a concrete example of that.[15]

The emotional scars inflicted on Donnelly by the controversy were deep. When queried by a newspaper feature writer whether he would ever again take a stand for a controversial belief that clashed with mainstream public opinion, he replied, "Never!"

The anger and frustration of Rhode Islanders was vented in letters to the editor of the *Pawtucket Evening Times*. Portions of three letters are typical of the month-long succession of citizen reaction.

Let's take our hats off to our courageous and outspoken Mayor. It is a sad commentary when the ACLU can disrupt one of the greatest holidays, hiding behind the First Amendment. Mayor Lynch you are not alone in this fight. Millions of God-fearing people are on your team.[16]

Nativity Scenes have been a part of Christmas displays for centuries. When the Church sanctifies this occasion, you cannot separate church and state, any fool knows that. Are they [ACLU] secretly striving for communism? We will pray for their souls, as they sure need it.[17]

I am enraged and I am not going to take it any longer. I wish to register my protest in the name of a segment of the long-suffering silent majority. I am really disillusioned by the court's attempt to defend the strident few at the expense of the convictions of the silent majority. The question is who is being protected from what and who is being persecuted? Please Christians and Jews of Rhode Island, voice your protest against this callous nitpicking![18]

Not surprisingly, leaders of the religious community in Rhode Island entered into the dispute. Protestant clergy, particularly fundamentalists, took to the pulpits to defend the city. The Reverend Eunio Cugini, of the Clayville Baptist Church, argued that "when anybody attacks Christianity and nibbles away, eventually the whole structure of American society is threatened. This is a Christian country. We invite all men to take residence here. But one condition of that residency is that they respect our traditions. These are a part of America and we feel that whoever comes in has an obligation to respect them, to become familiar with them, and to abide by them." [19]

The Visitor, the official newspaper of the Roman Catholic diocese of Rhode Island, ran an editorial entitled "We Congratulate Mayor Lynch." It stated, in part:

> We commend Mayor Lynch for refusing to dismantle the Nativity Scene and disconnect the sound system. Everyone agrees that many American traditions have their origin in religion. And everyone agrees that many of the traditions with the passing of time have assumed an identity of their own. They have become secular traditions. The Nativity Scene and Christmas carols are in this category. The American Constitution is not violated when a city tries to brighten parks and attract shoppers by putting up some Christmas decorations. [20]

Although public support for the ACLU was noticeably absent at the outset of the dispute, it was from a group of Protestant ministers that the strongest sentiment for separation of church and state emerged. Thirty-one pastors issued a public statement, which said:

> While festivities, lights, and generations of good will in this season have roots in both religion and secular traditions, the creche is a specifically religious symbol. Our coun-

try, while deeply influenced by a Judeo-Christian heritage, is not itself Judeo-Christian but is pluralistic, consisting of many rich religious traditions and recognizing the value of all. Government in our country, wisely recognizing the diversity of these traditions, was set up to steer clear of embracing any while protecting the religious freedom of all.

We as pastors have a responsibility to educate our people in the history of religious strife and the futility of imposing religious beliefs on the human conscience. The specifically religious observance of this holiday belongs in our homes, and in our churches and synagogues. Although there are public recognitions of this glad season, they should be confined to those symbols and traditions which are not identified with any one group.[21]

Throughout the six weeks prior to the district court trial, the most prolific spokesmen for the opposing sides of the Nativity scene dispute were Brown for the ACLU and Mayor Lynch for Pawtucket. From their public appearances, newspaper accounts, and personal interviews, the contours of the debate gradually evolved. Both men felt very strongly about their position. Insight into their personal backgrounds and a composite account of their public statements about the case shed considerable light on the difficult questions raised by the city's display of the creche and other church–state issues.

WITNESS FOR THE PLAINTIFF: THE ACLU POSITION

The American Civil Liberties Union was founded in 1920 to protect individual rights and to promote the concept of limited government. It subscribes to the view that even in a democracy the elected government is not permitted to take away from the people "the inherent right to freedom of expression, belief, and association, to procedural fairness, to equal treatment before the law, to privacy."[22] It relies heavily on litigation, legislative lobbying, and public education to achieve its results. A champion of minority causes, its stands are often unpopular and frequently misunderstood by the general public.

In its first major case in 1925, the ACLU defended John Scopes, the Tennessee biology teacher who introduced his students to theories of evolution despite the state's official endorsement of the biblical view of creation. The battle to prohibit states from imposing religious doctrines on public school children continues to this very day. A 1987 Supreme Court decision struck down a Louisiana statute that forbade the teaching of evolution unless it was accompanied by instruction in "creation science."[23]

Throughout the last half-century the ACLU has worked to secure the freedom of speech and association for labor union organizers, to protect the rights of Japanese Americans quarantined during World War II, and to resist the efforts to enforce political conformity, which spread across the nation during the McCarthy era in the 1950s. Civil rights activists, conscientious objectors, antiwar demonstrators, welfare recipients, mental patients, and prisoners have all benefited from the ACLU's efforts.

Support for the ACLU and its positions can become a political liability. In the 1988 presidential campaign George Bush worked hard to convince voters that because Michael Dukakis was a "card-carrying" member of the organization, he was clearly out of the mainstream of American politics. Most Americans probably agreed with the vice-president's characterization, at least as far as it pertained to the ACLU.

Although Donnelly became identified in the case name as the plaintiff in the Nativity scene suit, the major force behind the ACLU action was Brown. Brown, who is Jewish, attended Hebrew school for approximately ten years. His interest in civil liberties was awakened by his religious upbringing and by the authoritarian nature of the Philadelphia public high school he attended. Graduated with a degree in political science from Vassar College, his academic training stimulated an interest in First Amendment issues. Part-time work with the Philadelphia office of the ACLU led him first to a position with the Ohio affiliate and eventually to Des Moines, Iowa, where he became executive director of the Iowa chapter in 1979.

It was in Iowa that Brown experienced church–state conflict firsthand. The ACLU was successful in persuading the city of Des Moines to stop its Christmas Nativity pageant, in which city employees were recruited to act out the roles. When Pope John Paul II traveled to Iowa in October 1979, the ACLU successfully challenged towns that had planned to use school buses to transport residents to a Catholic Mass celebrated by the pope. When the organization protested Des Moines' decision to close down city government in honor of the pontiff's visit, the federal district court first supported the ACLU's protest, but relented when the city argued that the closings were related to matters of health and safety, not support for religion.

Brown accepted an offer to come to Rhode Island in 1980, a few short months before the Nativity scene suit was initiated. He and a secretary work out of meager quarters in an unrefurbished downtown Providence office building. The office is cluttered with endless piles of papers, books, and pamphlets that attest to the importance of the ACLU's educational mission in the community. Although he frequently finds himself on the unpopular side of the issues that take up his time, Brown does not come across as vindictive or as the "troublemaker" his public image sometimes conveys. He has a clear sense of his own mission and the goals of the organization. He realizes that the small steady gains that are made, even in losing causes, are as important to his work as the major victory he sought in bringing the Pawtucket case to court.

Brown describes the ACLU position on the Nativity scene case with the following statement:[24]

After I received a phone call from a Pawtucket woman who objected to the Nativity scene in Hodgson Park, I visited the display on two occasions. I was offended by it. To me it signified the birth of Christ. I was upset that the city was sponsoring and endorsing the most fundamental tenet of Christianity, the acceptance of Jesus as the Messiah. I believe very strongly in the First Amendment principles of separation of church and state. I do not believe that government has any business involving itself in religion.

The Founding Fathers decided that keeping government and religion as two separate and distinct spheres was the best way of protecting both government and religion. It protects government by removing it from very controversial religious issues, from being torn apart by having to take sides. By remaining completely neutral, government can represent all of the people.

Mayor Lynch's press conference at the site of the Nativity scene on the day after the suit was filed illustrates why separation of church and state is so important. His actions show the political divisiveness that can occur when government gets involved in religion. The First Amendment was designed to keep government officials from making religion a political issue. In this case Pawtucket is taking sides in a religious matter. It is approving a religious idea and symbol to the detriment of religious minorities, nonbelievers, and even to Christians who object to government involvement. Although many persons have complained that the ACLU action is a trival matter, the uproar that has been created shows that the issue goes to the heart of basic beliefs.

The charges that the ACLU position is the antireligious view of nonbelievers is not true. On the contrary, the separation of church and state protects religion and our religious diversity. Both minority and majority faiths are benefited. When the majority is allowed to use the power of the state on their behalf, the minority operates at a disadvantage. They are persecuted. This is especially true when tax money is involved. It is totally inappropriate to use taxes, which are collected from all the people, to promote a particular religion.

The psychological effect on members of minority religions, particularly children, is also very real. When government expresses a religious point of view with which they are unfamiliar or do not agree, they feel left out. And that is really what is happening when the government puts up a creche. Minorities are left out and in a psychological sense are ostracized from the community.

We often lose sight of the fact that the First Amendment also means to protect majority religions from being politicized by government. When government gets involved in religion two things can happen. First, when you invite government aid, you also invite government interference. More important to this case is the fact that government involvement promotes the secularization of religion. Religion is ultimately degraded and cheapened when it relies on government and government officials to spread its faith; it necessarily loses some of its independence.

The Pawtucket display illustrates this when you see that the Nativity scene is surrounded by Santa Claus, reindeer, and even an elephant. When religious symbols are used for political or community purposes, they end up losing their religious significance. I think that any truly religious person would want to be careful to see that their sacred symbols are not misused and appropriated by government officials for their own purposes.

In bringing this suit the ACLU was trying to make a statement about a constitutional issue with implications that transcend the Nativity scene and the city of Pawtucket. Rhode Island is the most Catholic state in the Union. In this situation and in other areas of the country where you can have such a large majority of the same religion, it can breed an unconscious insensitivity to the notion of separation of church and state. We cannot let the unpopularity of our position deter us from taking what to us is a clear-cut constitutional stand. Almost by definition, defending civil liberties is taking an unpopular stand on behalf of minorities. Majorities generally don't need protection from the government because they are the ones running the government.

It should also be pointed out that the ACLU supports individuals' First Amendment rights to worship as they please. It's the opposite side of the same coin. The First Amendment, which prohibits government from sponsoring a Nativity display with city money, also protects the individual's right to put up a Nativity Scene on their lawns and in their churches without government interference. We are not opposed to Nativity scenes, we are opposed to government sponsorship of Nativity scenes. When citizens are free to practice religion as they wish, is it fair for the government to step in and put the weight of authority behind one particular belief or symbol? I think not. When church and state mix, religion is often debased and government's authority as representative of all the people is seriously undermined.

FOR THE DEFENSE: THE MAYOR RESPONDS

Dennis M. Lynch is a lifelong Pawtucket resident. Born to an Irish Roman Catholic family of modest means, he was educated in his local parish grammar school and graduated from St. Raphael's Academy. He received his undergraduate degree from Providence College and attended Boston College law school for two years, after which he returned to his home town to operate a real estate and insurance business. Reared by a family that took its community and civic responsibility seriously, Lynch ventured into city politics in 1973, when he was elected mayor. A Democrat, he was reelected four times. Often mentioned as a prospective candidate for governor or congressman, the mayor resigned his office in 1981 to become Rhode Island state purchasing agent, a position he still holds. Lynch and his wife Irene raised seven children. The family continues to reside in Pawtucket, four blocks from the home where the former mayor was born.

Lynch comes across as a man devoted to the values of family and community. The pictures, mementos, and awards that grace the walls of his state office testify to the pride he holds for his children and for his service as mayor. Pawtucket is family to Lynch, and one is left with the impression that he approached his mayoral duties in much the same manner a father assumes responsibility for his family.

Traditions are important, too. Lynch talks fondly of the childhood experiences that shaped his values and that continue to color his views of the world. The decline of the family unit and the erosion of traditional values are troubling. For Mayor Lynch and many of his generation in Pawtucket, nationalizing trends in American society are today challenging the "familiar" and undermining "tradition." The former mayor brought the following perspective to the Nativity scene controversy: [25]

> My first reactions to the suit were anger and frustration. I was mad. The suit was ridiculous. With vital concerns about jobs, taxes, inflation, and nuclear war on our political agenda, why did we have to argue over a community tradition that no one found offensive, except the ACLU? It's something that is happy and joyous and helps to overcome what is to some persons a letdown during the holiday season. This was our thought behind the Nativity scene and the full Christmas display.
>
> Some of my earliest memories are of my mother taking

my brothers and I to the display. When I was eleven years old, the same year my mother passed away, my father asked me to go with him to bring some live sheep that he had loaned to the city that were to be included in the display. With a spirit of joy, peace, and happiness we added our family's contribution to the celebration. That was forty years ago. We are talking about a tradition that has existed in the community for a long, long time.

As mayor of the city, do you expect to be ordered to censor the truth, to remove the elements of a national holiday? We all recall two sad and pathetic characters, Scrooge and the Grinch who stole Christmas. No matter how they twist the words, these are the characters of sadness, intolerance, and insensitivity played out by the ACLU.

Actually, I was not completely surprised by the suit. Every year a representative from the organization would stop by my office to complain about the outdoor display and my office decorations. Just before his death, my uncle, who was a parish priest, gave me a small Nativity scene, which I displayed in my outer office. It became something of an office joke to speculate how long it would take for the ACLU to register their protest. Each year I steadfastly refused their request to remove the displays. I told them that this is a great and free society and that everybody has a right to sue. In 1980 they did not come back; they sued. I was forced into court on behalf of seventy-one thousand Pawtucket residents to defend a century-old tradition. It didn't make sense.

When I phoned my wife to tell her about the suit and warn her of the impending media blitz, her response was, "You're not going to let them get away with it, are you?" We both knew that this was something I would fight to the bitter end. My political instincts told me that the great majority of my constituents would back my decision to fight, but that really didn't matter. Some said that was why I was fighting and I wanted to use the issue as a political springboard, but obviously from the record, I never did. The point is, though, that you could never have forecast how many people of good will nationwide got upset and supported our stand.

In order to help get the message across and enlist community support, I held an impromptu press conference next to the Nativity scene. It was a very emotional time for me. A crowd of about seventy-five persons, including representatives of the media, gathered for the noontime rally. I spoke about the action that had been taken and the importance of the display to the city. We sang Christmas carols. At one point I passed among a group of school children who had come to view the display and I let some of them sing into my microphone. The group included some slow learners, one of whom asked me, "Don't they know it isn't Christmas without this?"

I was roundly criticized by the ACLU for politicizing the issue. But the event helped me to dramatize just what it was I was trying to protect. I couldn't believe the tremendous outpouring of support we received. Letters and phone calls poured in from all over the country praising my actions. I was gratified that even some from the Jewish community in Pawtucket rallied to my defense and support. Their response was an indication that they considered the Nativity scene not as a religious symbol, but as an indication of good will and community tradition.

One of the reasons my ancestors came to the United States was to escape religious persecution and to live in a country where they were guaranteed freedom of speech and religion. These freedoms have made this country strong. Two hundred years of historical experience have proven that. As a result of the ACLU suit the people of Pawtucket have banded together to renew those views and to claim the rights for their children and grandchildren. They resent the ACLU setting up another form of religion, a secular non-religion, if you will, and foisting it upon the community.

The effect of the challenge to the Nativity scene is the undermining of the rights of every child to freedom of expression. Do the majority of the people in a democracy have any rights? I think they do. I fought for the right of any community in our land to either have or not have such a tradition.

I found it strange that the ACLU was supporting a practice which happens only in totalitarian states like the Soviet Union, where public religious displays are forbidden. It is strange that in their haste to prevent public displays, including Nativity scenes, that in their anxiety to do away with such things, they actually establish a secular non-religion. That is a very dangerous position, which exists only in totalitarian states.

We believe in the tradition of historical fact. No one challenged me on whether Christ was born 1,980 years ago. This is what we celebrate. It is important for us not to back away from or censor historical fact. I find it rather amusing that the ACLU could take a position where they oppose censorship yet they are asking us to remove the manger scene. They are asking us to remove the person from his own birthday party, and change historical fact. That is censorship.

Where in the world did the Founding Fathers of the Constitution say that you shall not have a Nativity scene, that you shall not have the freedom of expression? That is all we are talking about. People resent someone trying to impose another kind of religion on them. That is not what the Constitution means.

Religion has always played a vital part in American life, and it frequently spills over into matters of government. When I enter the court, I will pass through its portals on which God's name is plastered all over its marble exterior. I will be required to tell the whole truth, "so help me God." I will pay for parking with coins inscribed with "In God We Trust." Presidential proclamations endorse national days of prayer and commemorate Thanksgiving as a day set aside to thank God.

As a matter of fact, nowhere in the Constitution or in a Supreme Court decision has anyone ever mandated that a local community must divorce or separate religion from its public displays, and it is a fallacy to try to tell the public that this is what the Constitution means. We do not establish religion with a Nativity scene. It is intellectually dishonest to say to the city that the First Amendment prevents them from acknowledging one of the most important elements of Christmas.

It is also important to recognize that despite the association of the Nativity scene with the Christian religion, less than 1 percent of the total area of Pawtucket's Christmas display is devoted to the manger scene. To concentrate on that part of the display ignores the holiday context in which it is situated. The carousel, Santa Claus house, and other holiday figures dominate the display. I do not think that most people look at our Christmas display in religious terms. I consider the Nativity scene as an important part of the celebration, but not the main theme or primary reason for the display.

The Nativity scene, in the context of the total display, is important to the city's Christmas celebration for reasons other than religion. First, it is part of the community's culture and traditions. Second, it is aesthetically an attractive part of the display. And along with other parts of the display, it contributes to the economic well-being of the city.

The Christmas display must be considered along with the whole range of activities that the city undertakes to recognize the culture and traditions of the community. As mayor, I have tried to revitalize community spirit by involving a great many organizations and individuals in the downtown area on national and state holidays. The city has joined in concert with the business community to plan these kinds of events throughout the year on a regular basis to promote downtown Pawtucket. Part of the reason for moving the display to the central city was to assist with its redevelopment and to coordinate the city's Christmas observance with the activities of merchants.

Keep in mind that people can visit the Christmas displays without believing in anything. We hold no religious services there. No one approaches them to talk about religion. It is simply an opportunity to join with their brothers and sisters in the community in what should be a joyous time of the year and expressions of good will to all. What we are saying is that we have a right to gather as a community to express ourselves in this manner. This is a very important part of the American way of life.

I will not accept an interim judgment that says the manger scene has to come down and cannot be put up in the city of Pawtucket. I will not accept that. If you recall the movie *Network,* the underlying theme of that film was that the reporter was able to use the press to bring people together to express their frustrations. "I am mad and I'm not going to take it anymore," they chanted. Well, that is what is happening in Pawtucket. The people are mad as hell and are not going to take it anymore. One way or another a tradition like this is going to survive. No judge, no jury is going to undermine that.

THE TRIAL

The formal proceedings in *Donnelly v. Lynch* began on 3 February 1981 in Providence federal district court with a fact-finding trial presided over by Judge Pettine. Representing the ACLU in the case were attorneys Amato A. DeLuca and Sandra A. Blanding of Revens & DeLuca Ltd., a Warwick, Rhode Island, law firm. DeLuca, whose firm works for no fee (*pro bono*) in ACLU cases, had represented the Rhode Island affiliate in other legal actions. On the advice of the city solicitor, Mayor Lynch retained the firm of MacMahon and MacMahon of Providence. William F. MacMahon is recognized for his work in constitutional law cases.

Testimony was received from ten individuals during the three-day trial.[26] Photographs and diagrams of the display, written communications received by the mayor in connection with the suit, letters to the editor, and newspaper clippings were also introduced into evidence. Although the display had been removed from Hodgson Park shortly after the New Year, Judge Pettine and the principals visited the site.

City Finance Director Mumford and Parks Director Dufault explained the financial and logistical relationships of the Nativity scene to the overall display. They testified that the creche occupied approximately 140 square feet of the 40,000-square-foot area covered by the display. Funds expended by the city on the Nativity scene since its purchase for $1,375 in 1973 had been minimal. Each year two city workers worked approximately one hour each to assemble and remove the creche. It was estimated that of the $4,500 in employee wages associated with the construction and dismantling of the total display, only $20 was attributable to the Nativity scene. A small sum, approximately $20, was spent for spotlights and light bulbs, and an indeterminate sum for electricity was also expended.

In their questioning and cross-examination of witnesses,

ACLU attorneys elicited testimony to support their contention that the manger scene was a purely religious symbol without secular meaning and that its purpose was to promote the religious views of the majority. Plaintiffs also attempted to show that the controversy precipitated harmful political and social divisions among the city's residents. By reinforcing a notion that America is a Christian country, the city's actions relegated nonbelievers and citizens who belonged to other religious faiths to an inferior position in the community.

Donnelly stated in his testimony that, unlike the Santa Claus and other secular items in the Christmas display, which are not mentioned or described in the Bible or other religious literature, the creche attempts "to tell a complete story in itself, the story of the birth of Christ." Methodist minister Thomas Ramsbey added to Donnelly's characterization of the scene.

> It is clearly Christian symbolism because it relates only to the birth of Christ. Moreover, the symbols that go with it, the figures are kneeling in worshipful attitude, even the animals are standing in a worshipful pose. . . . The angels represent messengers from heaven, they deliver good news to the people, and therefore the whole setting of the creche is a statement about the divinity if you will or the extraordinariness of the birth of this baby Jesus. It is no ordinary baby and that's very clear from the symbols that are there.
>
> I was appalled by the fact that here was a very sacred religious symbol to Christianity being erected by the City in conjunction with a lot of other symbols that clearly were not specifically Christian and I felt it took away from or demeaned the Christian symbol in that setting.

In their questioning of Brown and Lynch, plaintiff attorneys attempted to show that most of the individuals who reacted adversely to the suit viewed the Christmas display in religious terms and interpreted the ACLU's action as an attack on the religious views of the majority. Brown testified that on the basis of phone calls, letters, and public appearances it was his impression that the majority of individuals did not view the issue raised by the suit as a trivial matter; they clearly thought the city was entitled to sponsor the religious traditions of the Christian community.

Mayor Lynch first testified that the creche was central to the Christmas display for cultural, aesthetic, and economic reasons. Later in his testimony the mayor modified his position by stating that the manger scene was incidental and not the primary focus of the overall display. Pressed throughout the questioning whether he would erect a display without the Nativity scene should the courts strike it down, the mayor grudgingly admitted that he would do so. He went on to note, however, that citizens would be angry if the creche had to go. "The bringing of the suit was a very divisive thing in the community and that divisiveness had never, and I am a lifelong resident of the community, had never been seen in my community before."

Expert testimony on the nature and effect of the Nativity scene on non-Christians was presented by Michael Werle, a licensed clinical psychologist. In response to questions from ACLU attorneys he offered the following testimony.

> I think that the Nativity scene is a very powerful religious symbol because it is . . . clearly a symbol of the worship of Jesus. My concern is that when young children who would be very attracted by the display . . . go into such an environment they are totally open to that environment, it's magical to them. They don't think about it, they simply experience it so that the impressions that are made on the child under those experiences are very, very vivid. That's what makes it fun and that's why parents like to do it.
>
> The problem with such a symbol for someone who is not Christian, either a non-believer or another faith, is that it

raises profound questions for that child insofar as whether or not he is okay, or more importantly, whether his parents are okay, because unlike a Nativity scene in a churchyard where a child might ask what that is and the parents can say that's the symbol of the worship of Jesus which is a part of the Christmas celebration, in a public setting the question has to be raised for the child as to whether they are in fact part of the culture represented.

I think the responses to this suit in the paper which I've been reading and the letters to the editor visibly illustrate how important the Nativity scene is to folks, how dearly they hold it. Santa Claus, Christmas trees, even gift giving are done in non-Christian families, in non-believing families all over the country, but the Nativity scene has a different aspect and different tradition. . . . It evokes a sense of identification problem. Who am I, what do I belong to, am I part of this country, or am I part of my family and is that in conflict?

I also believe it encourages religious chauvinism. For an adult to see such a symbol reinforces an already prevalent attitude in our country that we are a Christian country . . . and it's only a step from there to believing that other religions and people who are of other persuasions are somewhat less important and have less merit so it encourages people who already confuse being American with being Christian. It makes that confusion more difficult for them to see.

At the outset of their presentation the defense raised an important procedural question for Judge Pettine to consider. Counsel for Pawtucket challenged Donnelly's standing as a Pawtucket taxpayer, questioning whether he was a bona fide resident of the city, legally entitled to bring the complaint. In dispute was whether Donnelly ever paid $9.50 in property taxes on a car registered in his name. Financial records showed that this sum was the only tax bill ever received by the plaintiff and that it had not been paid. Unless it could be demonstrated that Donnelly as an interested party to the suit had paid taxes to the city and was consequently "harmed" by expenditures on the Nativity scene, the court could deny "standing to sue," which would cause the case to be dismissed on procedural grounds and avoid the necessity of reaching a decision on the merits.

The defense's substantive case was argued primarily on the basis that the city's sponsorship of a large Christmas display that included a Nativity scene did not violate the Establishment Clause because the total display was dominantly secular in purpose, context, and effect. Attorney MacMahon's cross-examination of Brown produced the following interchange, which illustrates the critical importance of "context" to the city's position.

MACMAHON: Now does the Madonna have a religious significance to you?

BROWN: Yes, it does.

MACMAHON: Does the Christmas tree have a religious significance?

BROWN: No, it doesn't.

MACMAHON: Do figurines of sheep and other animals have a religious significance to you?

BROWN: When viewed in the context of a Nativity Scene display, they certainly do.

MACMAHON: So you say that the significance of a symbol must be viewed in context, is that correct, that's your testimony isn't it?

BROWN: I'm saying that a Nativity Scene is one thing in and of itself in that it doesn't make sense to try to break it down as you're trying to do.

MACMAHON: Well, I'd like an answer to my question.

Your testimony is, is it not, that each component of the Nativity Scene must be viewed in context, isn't that your testimony?

BROWN: I don't believe so. I'm simply saying that you're right that there is nothing religiously significant in and of itself of a particular animal. That is correct, I will agree to that.

MACMAHON: Now there are also figurines representing a male figure, presumably a father, and a female figure, presumably a mother, correct?

BROWN: Yes.

MACMAHON: Now in and of themselves they have no religious significance, is that correct?

BROWN: In and of themselves the figure of a father and mother do not have religious significance, that is correct.

MACMAHON: So your testimony is that the religious significance is derived from all of those elements in context, isn't that a fair statement of your testimony?

BROWN: When all the elements, when they are all put together as a Nativity Scene display, that is correct.

MACMAHON: Okay, now it is also true that the Nativity Scene, as part of a secular display, must also be viewed in context, isn't that a fair statement.

BROWN: Not necessarily.

MACMAHON: So your testimony is that the elements of the Nativity Scene must be taken in combination but that the Nativity Scene is not to be taken in combination with other elements of the display, is that your testimony?

BROWN: Well, no, it's not that the elements of the Nativity Scene must be taken in combination, it's that one of those symbols in and of themselves are not necessarily religious but when more and more are added together they certainly do become a religious message and that's not changed by the fact that it may be surrounded by other displays that are not necessarily religious. It still is a religious display.

Another defense witness, Dr. David Freeman, a University of Rhode Island philosophy professor, was more sympathetic to MacMahon's argument about the context of the manger scene in the total city display. Freeman, whose scholarship touches the area of symbolism, testified that a religious symbol like the creche "doesn't occur in a vacuum, it occurs in a context. A symbol in a religious context would be a religious symbol and have a religious impact. A symbol in a non-religious context will not be a religious symbol and will not have a religious impact. A creche displayed in a church would definitely make a religious statement. In Hodgson Park, it is merely part of the whole."

Mayor Lynch testified that the primary purpose of the Christmas display was to foster community morale. Likening it to the city's Fourth of July, Memorial Day, and Veterans Day festivities, he did not believe that the average Pawtucket citizen considered the Christmas display to be a religious experience.

Two local merchants reiterated the mayor's emphasis on the importance of the Christmas celebration to redevelopment efforts in the inner city. The display was believed to be a key link in bringing commerce into the city. Up to 25 percent of retail business trade in the downtown area occurred between Thanksgiving and Christmas. Neither businessman, one of whom was Jewish, objected to the Nativity scene or had heard any complaints about it. Both men agreed on cross-examination, however, that the display's business impact would probably not be affected by the removal of the creche.

After more than ten hours of testimony, the trial was adjourned on 6 February 1981. Judge Pettine was left to ponder the evidence and come to a decision.

II

ROUND ONE: The District Court Decides

The system is designed to maximize the judge's anxiety, that he has just made a mistake or is about to. . . . When we judges get a question, it is almost always very important, and a tough case that is close enough to drive one mad. Hence the craft is hard.

> Irving R. Kaufman, U.S. Court of Appeals
> Judge for the Second Circuit

THE U.S. CONSTITUTION PLACES courts and judges in a unique position in the political system and makes special demands upon the way they function. The judiciary is the most independent of the three branches of government. Federal judges are appointed and hold their offices for life, barring misconduct. Without the electoral concerns of the president and members of Congress, a judge is positioned to exercise the power of judicial review mostly free of the influences that affect political decisions made outside the courtroom. In the judicial arena minority rights are as important as majority rule. Long-term implications of policy can be weighed against the passions of the moment. Constitutional limits on power may transcend the political wisdom that prompts some governmental activities.

It would be easy to mistake the judiciary's unique perspective and its special role as interpreter of the Constitution as nonpolitical, above ordinary politics. While it is true that courts' agendas are largely limited to disputes arising under the Constitution, statutes, and treaties, very few of the important political questions that have engaged Americans during our first two hundred years have escaped the attention of the courts. The Civil War, the income tax, economic depression, segregation, and abortion are but a few examples. The results of these cases cut to the heart of American politics. Judicial decisions help the political system to referee the struggle among groups for power, to authoritatively shape society's values, to influence "who gets what, when, and where," and to forge the compromise and consensus, which are the politician's art.

THE DISTRICT COURT

The only court specifically created by the Constitution was the Supreme Court. Article III, Section I stipulates that "the judicial power of the United States shall be vested in one Supreme Court, and in such inferior Courts as the Congress may from time to time ordain and establish." District courts were created by Congress in the Judiciary Act of 1789.

At the beginning of their existence, the jurisdiction of district courts was not broad. Most of their cases dealt with maritime disputes. It was assumed that state courts, bound by the Supremacy Clause (Article VI), would enforce the Constitution as the "supreme law of the land." However, when those who desired a strong national government concluded that the state courts were not going to be vigorous enough in the enforcement of national law, the federal court system expanded and its jurisdiction grew. One result of that process was that district courts emerged as the dominant federal courts of original jurisdiction.[1]

Today district courts are still the basic trial courts of general federal law. Both civil and criminal cases are heard. All suits at this level are being tried for the first time; district courts hear no cases on appeal.[2] Only one judge sits on most cases.[3] Civil matters constitute about 85 percent of the docket, which now approaches a quarter of a million cases annually. Antitrust, commerce, environmental protection, job discrimination, and prison conditions are included among the diverse range of cases. Most criminal cases tried in district court relate to matters concerning constitutional rights of defendants. Accelerated crime rates in recent years, particularly in the area of drug-related offenses, has added to the district court's caseload in criminal matters.

There are 575 judges who preside over the 94 federal district courts in the United States (Figure 1). Because of the rapidly expanding workload, Congress has more than doubled the number of district judgeships since 1960. Most states, like Rhode Island, have one district court; some of the larger states have as many as four. The number of judges in each district varies from 2 to 27 depending on the caseload. Four judges, including Judge Pettine at the time of *Donnelly v. Lynch,* serve on the Rhode Island court.

Although district court judges are constitutionally appointed by the president and confirmed by the Senate, the practice of "senatorial courtesy" dictates that presidents seek the advice of senators from their own party in the state where the appointment is to be made.[4] (In the situation where there is no senator from the president's party, state party leaders or other elected officials are often consulted.) In practice the president is seldom directly involved in the selection of district judges. The justice department routinely works with the appropriate senators, the Federal Bureau of Investigation, and the American Bar Association in screening judicial candidates.[5]

The selection criteria for federal judges has come under close scrutiny in recent years. The political loyalties of the proposed judges have long been regarded as the major factor in the

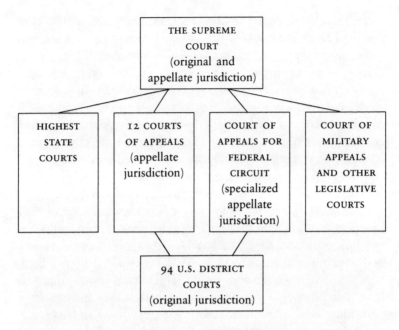

FIGURE 1. THE JUDICIARY IN THE UNITED STATES

selection process. In some instances the policy positions or the ideology of the nominee has been paramount. Many senators responded to Jimmy Carter's preference to use independent citizen-dominated merit commissions to identify qualified candidates for district court judgeships. Ronald Reagan, however, did not follow the Carter example. Because the circumstances surrounding each appointment are somewhat unique, generalizations are difficult to come by. It is safe to say that the process is imbued with a varying mix of patronage, political philosophy, and professionalism.

Judge Pettine brought a lifetime of experience in the law to the formidable task of weighing the evidence in *Donnelly v.*

Lynch against the First Amendment's Establishment Clause. With the exception of five years in the army during World War II (1941–1946), his entire adult life had been spent as an attorney, prosecutor, or judge. A lifelong resident of Rhode Island, Pettine was educated at Providence College. He received two law degrees from Boston University. Shortly after his release from active military duty he became special counsel to the Rhode Island attorney general (1948–1952), and then assistant attorney general (1952–1961). In 1961 President Kennedy appointed him U.S. attorney for Rhode Island, and in 1966 President Johnson nominated him for the position of judge of the U.S. District Court for Rhode Island. He became chief judge of the court in 1971.

Donnelly v. Lynch asked a lot from Judge Pettine. It was a "tough case," made more difficult by the fact that no similar dispute had been decided by a higher court. The "rule of precedent" was not particularly helpful. It is true that the district court setting sometimes "gives more scope to a judge's initiative and discretion."[6] However, the court of appeals and the Supreme Court, which are capable of overruling a lower court decision, are always looking over the shoulder of the district judge. Pettine believed that whatever he decided, the case would be appealed. He did not want to make a mistake.

Judges are not supposed to be affected by the possible public reaction to their decisions. Life tenure is thought to free them from this concern. However, Pettine knew that *Donnelly v. Lynch* was not an ordinary case. He had witnessed what he would later describe as "the horrifying arena of anger, hostility, name-calling, and political maneuvering" that accompanied the suit.[7] Just a year earlier he had been at the center of another major controversy when he ruled in favor of a homosexual high school student who had been denied permission to take another male student to his graduation prom.

Pettine suspected the public would be even more concerned with preserving government's right to display the Nativity scene than with preventing a gay couple from attending a school dance. Would his liberal reputation on controversial social issues get him into trouble? It would be easy to hide behind the cloak of the independent judiciary, but all judges know that if the public loses confidence in the ability of a judge or his or her court, their legitimacy and effectiveness are undermined.

And then there are the attitudes and beliefs that shape a judge's private life. Legal controversies often test a judge's ability not to let personal values interfere with the responsibility to uphold the Constitution.

Judge Pettine is a devout Roman Catholic. He attends Mass two or three times a week, often stopping before work to worship at St. Francis Chapel, a short distance from his Providence office. He was named Knight of St. Gregory by Pope Paul IV and was among the first lay persons to serve as local president of Serra, an international organization that helps to interest young men in the priesthood. During the Christmas season a Nativity scene occupies a prominent place in the Pettine home.

For the religious judge the principle of separation of church and state may have challenged a lifetime of strongly held emotional beliefs. Supreme Court justice William Brennan recently commented about the personal struggle that occurs when questions of religious beliefs become immersed in constitutional disputes. "I had an obligation under the Constitution which could not be influenced by any religious preference. As a Roman Catholic I might do as a private citizen what a Roman Catholic does, and that is one thing, but to the extent that that conflicts with what I think the Constitution means or requires, then my religious beliefs have to give way."[8]

Nine months elapsed from the day the fact-finding trial in *Donnelly v. Lynch* concluded in early February 1981 until Pettine would issue his Nativity scene decision. The judicial craft is not easy.

THE SUPREME COURT AND ESTABLISHMENT: THE PRE-*LYNCH* YEARS

Every federal judge takes an oath of office in which he swears to uphold the Constitution and the laws of the United States. After witnesses have testified and documents have been received into evidence, the judge must apply his reading of the law to the facts in the case before him. Because the Supreme Court is the highest court in the judicial system, judges look to its decision as the best authority on "settled law." So it was for Judge Pettine as he grappled with the constitutionality of a city-owned Nativity scene.

When they provided in the First Amendment that "*Congress shall make no law*," the Framers of the Constitution clearly meant it to apply to the national government. However, most cases involving the Establishment Clause, including *Donnelly v. Lynch,* relate to the actions of state and local governments. The Fourteenth Amendment, ratified in 1868, has provided the courts with the constitutional grounds to bring the states into conformity with national civil liberties standards. The text of the Amendment reads, in part, "nor shall any state deprive any person of life, liberty, or property, without the due process of law."

By a rule of constitutional interpretation known as the "doctrine of incorporation," the Supreme Court, beginning in 1925, gradually interpreted "liberty" in the Fourteenth Amendment to include most of the protections of the Bill of Rights.[9] The Court ruled in *Cantwell v. Connecticut,* 310 U.S. 296 (1940), for example, that the Free Exercise Clause imposed upon the states the same restraints as upon the national government. The assumption in *Cantwell* that the Establishment Clause would also be incorporated was affirmed in *Everson v. Board of Education,* 330 U.S. 1 (1947).

Not all judges or constitutional scholars are in agreement that the Fourteenth Amendment was the proper way to expand federal court jurisdiction over the activities of state and local governments. A lengthy debate over the intentions of those who drafted the amendment has proved inconclusive. However, there are few individuals who expect the Court to pull back from their longstanding commitment to the doctrine of incorporation, and there is no evidence that the present Court is predisposed to overturn the *Everson* precedent.

Because most of the interaction between church and state in the United States has occurred in the area of education where state and local governments are supreme, the Supreme Court's concern with the Establishment Clause is a post-incorporation phenomenon.[10] Between 1947 and the point in 1981 when Judge Pettine was pondering his Nativity scene ruling, the Court decided nineteen cases in which actions of state and local government were alleged to violate the Establishment Clause (Table 1). The opinions in these cases set down a variety of standards to determine whether the Constitution has been violated. Unfortunately for Judge Pettine and other individuals who seek clarity in the law, the Supreme Court record appears "unsettled" and confused. The fact that each case entailed a unique set of circumstances that influenced the justices' reasoning makes it very difficult to apply existing Establishment law to new cases.

State Aid to Religious Schools: Everson *and* Allen

Two early decisions in the area of state aid to religion illustrate the fine line that often divides the Court. *Everson v. Board of Education* is the Court's most important establishment decision. For the first time it specifically applied the Establishment Clause to the states and set down a comprehensive definition of separation of church and state that all nine justices appeared to

TABLE 1. SUPREME COURT ESTABLISHMENT DECISIONS, 1947–1980

Case	Result*	Vote	Decision
Everson v. Board of Education 330 U.S. 1 (1947)	A	5–4	State reimbursement of cost of bus transportation to parochial schools approved.
McCollum v. Board of Education 333 U.S. 203 (1948)	S	8–1	Released time for religious instruction in public schools disallowed.
Zorach v. Clauson 343 U.S. 306 (1952)	A	6–3	Released time for religious instruction away from school premises approved.
McGowan v. Maryland 366 U.S. 420 (1961)	A	8–1	Sunday closing laws have a secular legislative purpose and do not tend to establish religion.
Engel v. Vitale 370 U.S. 421 (1962)	S	8–1	School prayers determined to be an impermissible method of promoting religion.
Abington Township v. Schempp 374 U.S. 203 (1963)	S	8–1	Recitation of Lord's Prayer and Bible reading in public schools disallowed.
Epperson v. Arkansas 393 U.S. 97 (1968)	S	9–0	Prohibition of use of texts teaching theories of evolution disallowed.
Board of Education v. Allen 392 U.S. 236 (1968)	A	6–3	State loan of secular texts to parochial school students upheld.
Walz v. Tax Commission 397 U.S. 644 (1970)	S	8–1	Tax exemptions for churches upheld to limit entanglement between church and state.
Lemon v. Kurtzman 403 U.S. 602 (1971)	S	9–0	State aid for religious school salaries promotes excessive government entanglement.

TABLE 1 *(continued)*

Case	Result*	Vote	Decision
Tilton v. Richardson 403 U.S. 672 (1971)	A	5–4	Construction grants to church-related colleges for non-religious buildings allowed.
Hunt v. McNair 413 U.S. 734 (1973)	A	6–3	Public revenue bond for non-sectarian facilities on religious campuses allowed.
Committee v. Nyquist 413 U.S. 756 (1973)	S	6–3	Tuition reimbursement and maintenance funds for parents and religious schools disallowed.
Levitt v. Committee 413 U.S. 472 (1973)	S	8–1	State support for testing and maintaining state-mandated records in church schools refused.
Meek v. Pittenger 421 U.S. 349 (1975)	S	5–4	State support to church schools for auxiliary services (e.g., counseling) disallowed.
Roemer v. Board of Public Works 426 U.S. 736 (1976)	A	5–3	Noncategorical grants to religious colleges for nonsectarian purposes upheld.
Wolman v. Walter 433 U.S. 229 (1977)	A	6–3	Diagnostic services by public school officials in church schools upheld.
Committee v. Reagan 444 U.S. 646 (1980)	A	5–4	State-mandated tests administered in church schools but graded by state officials upheld.
Stone v. Graham 449 U.S. 39 (1980)	S	5–4	State law that Ten Commandments be posted in public school classrooms disallowed.

* "A" refers to a decision that upheld government "accommodation of religion"; "S" indicates a "separationist" decision in which government aid, support, or acknowledgment of religion was disallowed.

accept. The case is probably more significant, however, for the "crack in the armor" it opened as the justices debated which forms of state aid to religious institutions are permitted by the First Amendment.

Everson concerned a New Jersey statute that authorized local school boards to reimburse parents for the costs of bus transportation to parochial schools. Plaintiffs challenged the law on the grounds that it permitted taxpayer money to support and maintain schools dedicated to the teaching of the Roman Catholic faith.

Writing for the majority, Justice Hugo Black, in an often cited passage, described the Court's understanding of the meaning of the Establishment Clause.

> The "establishment of religion" clause of the First Amendment means at least this: Neither state nor Federal Government can set up a church. Neither can pass laws which aid one religion, aid all religions or prefer one religion over another. Neither can force a person to go to or to remain away from church against his will or force him to profess a belief or disbelief in any religion. No person can be punished for entertaining or professing any religious beliefs or disbeliefs, for church attendance or non-attendance. *No tax in any amount, large or small, can be levied to support any religious activities or institutions, whatever they may be called, or whatever they may adopt to teach or practice religion.* [Italics added.] Neither a state nor the Federal Government can, openly or secretly, participate in the affairs of any religious organizations or groups and vice versa. In the words of Jefferson, the clause against establishment of religion by law was intended to erect "a wall of separation between Church and State."[11]

The opinion indicated general agreement that actual separation of church and state, and not merely the avoidance of a state religion or the favoring of one religion over another, was the guiding principle of the Establishment Clause. However, for many persons, including four dissenting justices, Black's application of the principle took an unexpected course. After erecting a high wall of separation, the majority sustained the New Jersey law as a valid exercise of the state's police power. In what has come to be known as the "child benefit theory," Black upheld the bus reimbursement plan on grounds that it was "public welfare legislation" designed not to benefit religion, but to help children get to school safely.[12]

For Justice Wiley Rutledge and three other dissenters, Black's decision to cast the ruling in terms of a "public welfare" program ignored the major constitutional issue.

> Does New Jersey's action furnish support for religion by use of the taxing power? Certainly it does, if the test remains undiluted as Jefferson and Madison made it, that money taken by taxation from one is not to be used or given to support another's religious training or belief, or indeed one's own. . . . The furnishing of contributions of money for the propagation of opinions which he disbelieves is the forbidden execution; and the prohibition is absolute for whatever measure brings that consequence and whatever amount may be sought or given to that end.[13]

What became clear from the *Everson* decision was that despite the broad interpretation of establishment in Black's opinion, the line of separation between church and state was an illusive one. The Court would need to devise better criteria to determine when aid to religion exceeds the limits of the Establishment Clause.

In the next state-aid-to-religion case, *Board of Education v. Allen*, 392 U.S. 236 (1968), the child benefit rationale was extended to support a New York law requiring local school boards to lend textbooks on nonreligious subjects without cost to parochial school students. In his majority opinion Justice Byron R. White accepted the argument that the plan was intended to benefit the children and their parents, not the religious schools. White then attempted to devise a test which would help to define the boundaries of constitutionality in this area. To be constitutional, he argued, the statute must have *a secular legislative purpose* and must have *a primary effect that neither advances nor inhibits religion.* Because the subject matter of the texts that were provided by the state were secular and not religious, and because it was possible to distinguish between the religious and secular parts of the education provided by the religious schools, the loan program was sustained.

Three dissenters, now including Justice Black, distinguished between nonideological support such as transportation, and books, which they argued were closely related to substantive religious views. They noted that in New York although the books were provided by public authorities, in actual practice it was the religious school personnel that selected the texts. Particularly troubling to the minority was the fact that the expansion of the child benefit theory now created the potential of massive government support for religious schools.[14]

Religion in the Public Schools: Released Time

The Court found similar difficulties in drawing constitutional limitations when religion entered the public schools. Two early rulings in this area concerned released-time programs. It was common for school districts across the country to make time available during the school day for students to participate in voluntary programs of religious instruction. In 1948 the Court reviewed a program in Champaign, Illinois, where religious teachers were permitted to come into the schools once a week to give religious instruction to students who elected to participate. Nonparticipants were given a study period. An atheist family challenged the program.

With only one justice dissenting, the Court ruled that the program was unconstitutional (*McCollum v. Board of Education*). The crucial fact for the majority was that the Champaign program involved the use of the school building for religious instruction. Speaking for the Court, Justice Black observed that "pupils compelled by law to go to school for secular education were released in part from the legal duty upon the condition that they attend religious classes. This is beyond all question a utilization of the tax established and tax supported public schools system to aid religious groups to spread their faith."[15]

In a separate concurring opinion, Justice Felix Frankfurter argued that because not all religious sects in the community were willing or able to participate in the program, the school system was actively advancing the religious views of some faiths at the expense of others. Even though the child was offered the option not to participate, it did "not eliminate the operation of influence by the school in matters sacred to conscience and outside the school's domain. The law of imitation operated; nonconformity is not an outstanding characteristic of children. The result [was] an obvious pressure upon children to attend."[16]

Four years later the Court retreated from its *McCollum* ruling by upholding a New York City released-time program. In a 6–3 decision, in which Justice William O. Douglas spoke for the majority, the Court decided that religious instruction taking place *during school time, but outside of the school building,* did not violate the Establishment Clause. Douglas observed:

> We are a religious people whose institutions presuppose a Supreme Being. . . . When the state encourages religious instruction or cooperates with religious authorities by adjusting the schedule of public events to sectarian needs, it follows the best of our traditions. For it then respects the religious nature of our people and accommodates the public service to their spiritual needs. To hold that it may

not would be to find in the Constitution a requirement that the government show a callous indifference to religious groups.[17]

Three dissenters, led by Justice Black, strongly disapproved of the use of the coercive power of compulsory education laws to pressure students into receiving religious instruction. The case was important, however, because it reaffirmed that in a difficult constitutional area with passionately competing viewpoints, the Court would resort to a pragmatic case-by-case approach to measure the subtle distinctions among the challenged practices. Equally important for succeeding courts, it established a precedent for government *accommodation* of religion that many judges and constitutional scholars allege was a significant departure from Black's definition of establishment in *Everson*.

Sunday Closing Laws

The constitutionality of Sunday closing laws reached the Court in the early 1960s. When the state enacts legislation requiring that certain businesses be closed on the Sabbath, is this a step toward creating an established church? The Court said no. What once had been a compulsory day of rest decreed by Christian religions to promote their beliefs and traditions had become over time a day of rest to promote public health, safety, and relaxation. A secular purpose had supplanted the original religious objectives of Sunday Laws.[18]

Although the decisions were well received by most religious groups, some constitutional scholars believed that the primary effect of the laws was to advance religion. The decisions also created "free exercise" problems for those individuals whose Sabbath is not on Sunday.[19] The immediate significance of the Sunday closing decisions for Judge Pettine, however, was whether the Supreme Court, which consented to a "secular" Sunday, might also be willing to extend the reasoning to apply to government's use of religious symbols such as a Nativity scene.

School Prayers and Bible Reading

The establishment decisions that aroused the most public interest and scorn related to school prayers and Bible readings. Having resisted school prayer challenges for almost thirty years, the Supreme Court ruled in 1962 that the twenty-two word, denominationally neutral, state-authored prayer that was repeated voluntarily by students in New York at the beginning of each school day was unconstitutional.[20]

A year later the Court overturned two state statutes that required the reading of passages from the Bible and the recitation of the Lord's Prayer in public schools. Whether denominationally neutral or voluntary, religious exercises prescribed as a part of the school curriculum for students compelled by law to attend school were a violation of the Establishment Clause. Justice Tom C. Clark, writing for the majority in the Bible-reading case, noted that

> the place of religion in our society is an exalted one,
> achieved through a long tradition of reliance on the home,
> the church, and the inviolable citadel of the individual
> heart and mind. We have come to recognize through bitter
> experience that it is not within the power of government to
> invade that citadel, whether its purpose or effect be to aid
> or oppose, to advance or retard. In the relationship be-
> tween man and religion, the State is firmly committed to a
> position of neutrality.[21]

Reaction to these decisions from members of Congress, the clergy, and the general public was negative and outspoken. The Court's critics applauded the words of Justice Potter Stewart, the lone dissenter in both cases, who carefully documented the impact of religion on our public ritual. Stewart cited references to God on our coins, in our nation's motto, in the "Pledge of Allegiance to the Flag," and the annual observance of a National Day of Prayer as evidence of the place of religion in the history and traditions of our people that are also reflected in our government.

Senator Sam Ervin's North Carolina Baptist upbringing moved him to observe that "the Supreme Court has made God unconstitutional." Francis Cardinal Spellman, spiritual leader of New York Catholics, lamented that the decisions "strike at the very heart of the godly tradition in which America's children have for so long been raised."[22] Repeated efforts to initiate a constitutional amendment to overturn the school prayer rulings failed, but the public outcry that resulted from the decisions insured that the Court, rather than put the establishment question to rest, would raise it to a heightened level of importance on the country's political and social agenda.

The Burger Court and the "Lemon Test"

One effect of the *Everson* and *Allen* decisions was to stimulate optimism among state and local education officials and religious authorities that other forms of direct financial aid to church schools would pass constitutional scrutiny. Rising education costs were imposing substantial financial burdens on parochial schools, and many states had come to the realization that subsidizing these schools would be less costly than absorbing their students into the public system. The result was an increase in cooperation between religious schools and the public sector. Not surprisingly, an increase in litigation over the burgeoning relationship also resulted.

Warren Burger, who succeeded Earl Warren as chief justice in 1969, assumed the major role in articulating the principles that would guide the Court's establishment decisions. In *Walz v. Tax Commission*, 397 U.S. 644 (1970), the Court sustained federal and state laws that exempted churches from paying property and income taxes. Writing for an 8–1 majority in his first establishment case, Burger argued that the exemptions for churches, as well as for other nonprofit organizations, provide beneficial and stabilizing influences for the community. These kinds of influences might be hampered or destroyed by the need to pay taxes.

The imposition of taxes on churches would foster "excessive government entanglement" with religion in disputes of property valuation, tax liens, and other financial matters. Exemption has a positive effect because it "restricts the fiscal relationship between church and state, and tends to complement and reinforce the desired separation insulating each from the other."[23]

The notion of "excessive government entanglement" reappeared a year later when in *Lemon v. Kurtzman*, 403 U.S. 602 (1971) the Court was asked to examine Rhode Island and Pennsylvania laws that provided teacher salary supplements, textbooks, and instructional materials to church schools. The Court unanimously struck down both laws and in the process specified the standards it would use to rule on subsequent establishment challenges.

The tripartite test that Justice Burger set down in *Lemon* stipulated that state aid to religious institutions was permissible only if it (1) had a secular legislative purpose; (2) had a primary effect that neither advanced nor inhibited religion; and (3) did not foster excessive government entanglement with religion. To determine whether government aid was "excessive" the Court would "examine the character and purpose of the institutions that are benefited, the nature of the aid that the State provided, and the resulting relationship between the government and the religious authority."[24]

The Rhode Island and Pennsylvania practices constituted "excessive government entanglement" because the states would need to monitor the teachers to ensure that their classes were totally secular and did not move into matters of religion. The reimbursement of church schools for textbooks and instructional materials also unconstitutionally advanced religion because, unlike in *Allen,* the aid was given directly to the schools rather than to the pupils or their parents.

The "Lemon Test," as it has come to be known, guided the Court's consideration of the increasing number of establishment challenges during Burger's tenure as chief justice. The pre-*Lynch* Burger Court issued eleven decisions (see Table 1). In six of the cases, the advocates of separation of church and state won. Government support of tuition reimbursement, field trip costs, maintenance and repairs, and auxiliary services such as psychological counseling were disallowed. The accommodationist point of view prevailed in five cases in which government aid for textbooks, public health and therapeutic services, and public support for the nonsectarian needs of religious colleges were found to satisfy *Lemon* standards.

The case coming the closest to raising the issue of religious symbolism that confronted Judge Pettine was the 1980 decision in which the Court ruled that a Kentucky law requiring the posting of a large reproduction of the Ten Commandments in every public classroom was unconstitutional. Even though the display carried a notation showing its secular applicability, the five-judge majority ruled that "the Ten Commandments are undeniably a sacred text in Jewish and Christian faiths, and no legislative recital of a secular purpose can blind us to the fact."[25] The underlying purpose of the law was to further a religious objective.

Not all constitutional scholars are convinced that the Lemon Test provides clear constitutional standards to adjudicate establishment questions. The subjectiveness of the tripartite guidelines limits their usefulness for lower court judges. Concepts such as "secular purpose," "primary" effect, and "excessive" entanglement leave considerable room for judicial discretion and debate. Even the Supreme Court's application of the test often turns on fine lines of distinction that more often than not produce sharply divided pluralities. Eight of the nine establishment rulings immediately following *Lemon* were decided by 5–4 or 6–3 votes.

Leonard W. Levy, one of the foremost scholars of religion and the Constitution, may have put his finger on the problem. "Tests have little to do with decisions: the use of a test lends the appearance of objectivity to a judicial opinion, but no evidence shows that a test influences a member of the Court to reach a decision that he would not have reached without that test. And, Justices using the same test often arrive at contradictory results."[26]

A QUESTION OF "STANDING"

To protect the integrity and orderliness of the judicial system and to secure the uniform application of the law, federal courts operate with well-defined rules of procedure. Before Judge Pettine would consider the merits of *Donnelly v. Lynch,* he had to resolve the jurisdictional question of "standing to sue" raised by Pawtucket's attorneys at the trial. Article III of the Constitution limits the courts' jurisdiction to cases and controversies "arising under this Constitution, the Laws of the United States and Treaties." Federal courts will not consider fictitious cases, suits for which there is no "injured" party; nor will they issue advisory opinions. The Supreme Court has ruled that "the gist of the question of standing is whether the party seeking relief has alleged such a personal stake in the outcome of the controversy as to assure that concrete adverseness . . . upon which the court so largely depends for illumination of difficult constitutional questions."[27]

Both the post-trial memorandum for the defense and an amicus curiae brief[28] submitted by Robert A. Destro on behalf of the Catholic League of Religious Rights urged the court to dismiss the suit on the basis that both Donnelly and the ACLU lacked standing. The trial record did not support Donnelly's status as a Pawtucket taxpayer. To challenge government expenditures under the First Amendment, plaintiffs are required to show injury by proving they had paid taxes that contributed to the costs of the practice to which they object. The testimony that Donnelly had paid approximately $9.50 in personal property taxes was contradicted by city financial records.

The ACLU position was also deficient. For the organization to claim taxpayer status it would have to demonstrate that it represented Pawtucket taxpayers who claimed to be injured by city expenditures for the Nativity scene. No taxpayers objecting to the display were identified at the trial.

The courts will sometimes grant standing if the injured party can demonstrate a sufficient noneconomic interest in a suit. Plaintiff attorneys argued that "Mr. Donnelly's 'spiritual stake in First Amendment values' and the injury which he suffered to those values as a result of the defendants' actions clearly constitute the type of non-economic injury sufficient to confer standing on Mr. Donnelly to bring the instant action."[29] Similarly they maintained that the ACLU had "representational standing" to bring the suit on behalf of its members who suffered the same injuries as Donnelly.

Professor Destro's amicus brief argued that a "spiritual stake in First Amendment" values alone is not enough to confer standing. He joined defense attorneys in urging the court not to "stretch the strained law of standing" by acknowledging "the tenuous and purely academic 'separationist' interest" demonstrated by the plaintiff.[30]

Tradition dictates that courts avoid involvement in cases that, for whatever reason, they feel it imprudent to hear. Judge Pettine was persuaded that both Donnelly and the ACLU lacked standing. Most judges would have exercised restraint and would have dismissed the suit on procedural grounds. Pettine, however, recognized that the case involved a controversial issue that would inevitably return to the court's docket. Pawtucket would continue to erect the Nativity scene. The ACLU would persist in its efforts to have it taken down. Some court would have to confront the question. Judge Pettine did not want to be accused of avoiding the issue.

On 31 August 1981 Pettine issued an unusual "tentative opinion" in which he warned both parties that unless the plaintiff position on standing could be corrected, the suit would have to be dismissed for lack of jurisdiction. He stated, in part:

> The sensitivity of this case and the great public and scholarly interest the litigation has generated must not obscure the underlying question of this Court's jurisdiction under Article III of the United States Constitution. The public's interest is best served by resolving, if at all possible, all threshold questions so as not to prevent the Court from deciding whether or not the Nativity Scene in the Hodgson Park Christmas Display violates the Establishment Clause of the First Amendment. To insure a resolution of this substantive question, for the first time, I am resorting to the rather novel approach of issuing a tentative ruling on the standing question.
>
> This past month I have spent a considerable number of hours studying the briefs, cases, and transcript; as I presently view the jurisdictional issue, it seems to me I am constrained to rule that the factual record does not establish that Mr. Donnelly has standing to litigate this case as a taxpaying resident of the City of Pawtucket. There can be no case or controversy within the framework of Article III if no taxpaying member joins this lawsuit.
>
> Now, of course, the standing question may be argued from another perspective: standing of the American Civil Liberties Union (ACLU) to litigate this action as an organizational representative of its members who are Pawtucket residents.

Conceding that ACLU Pawtucket taxpaying members who share the organization's belief that the display is offensive to their First Amendment rights might have standing, the fact remains that the record fails to identify any such person, and I do not believe I can assume such persons exist.

Going on, the question may be raised whether there is a sufficient non-economic interest in this litigation to satisfy any valid test of "injury in fact" so as to confer standing; that is, whether a "spiritual stake in First Amendment values" alone is enough to support standing. . . . Whether or not the United States Supreme Court will sustain such an open-ended theory of standing remains to be seen. I hesitate to enter into this complicated, difficult area.

I reiterate this is a tentative opinion. I am prepared to hear arguments on these points or, in the alternative, leave to counsel the future action they may wish to take. Of course, you have a right to stand on the record; if you do, a formal opinion will be filed.

Both parties to the case interpreted Judge Pettine's tentative decision as an invitation to explore ways of amending the suit to satisfy the question of standing. On 16 October 1981 ACLU attorneys, with the consent of the city, added three Pawtucket taxpayers and ACLU members to the suit. The way was now clear for Judge Pettine to consider the merits of the case.

POST-TRIAL MEMORANDA TO JUDGE PETTINE

At the conclusion of the district court trial, ACLU and Pawtucket attorneys submitted written briefs to Judge Pettine in defense of their constitutional positions. Because it was the prevailing judicial standard, both parties discussed the city's display of the Nativity scene from the perspective of the three-part criterion set down by the Supreme Court in *Lemon v. Kurtzman*.

Secular Purpose

The first requirement of the Lemon Test stipulates that the activity in question must have a secular legislative purpose if it is to survive an Establishment Clause challenge. To many viewers the Nativity scene, even when displayed in the context of a larger Christmas celebration, remained a strong symbol of Christianity. A recent court opinion held that "the State is not allowed to use religious means to serve secular ends where secular means would suffice."[31] Furthermore, in ruling against the posting of the Ten Commandments in public schools, the Supreme Court had viewed with skepticism the use of religious symbols to advance allegedly secular purposes.

The main question for the ACLU turned on whether the secular purposes of Pawtucket's Christmas display would be compromised if the Nativity scene were removed. Mayor Lynch and the Pawtucket merchants who testified indicated that the inclusion of the manger scene was incidental to the display. It neither added to nor subtracted from its secular purpose. Plaintiffs concluded that there was no secular purpose served by the Nativity scene which could not be served equally well by other clearly secular symbols.

The city's position was based primarily on the contextual setting of the Nativity scene in the total display. The dominant purpose of the display and each of its components was to celebrate Christmas, a secular national holiday, and to promote the downtown business district, both commercially and aesthetically. Finding a parallel with the Supreme Court's "secularization" of Sunday as a day of rest, defense attorneys argued that a celebration of Christmas that "includes a religious component ought not to constitute an establishment as long as the religious component is placed in its appropriate secular context."[32] Acknowledging that the creche retains more religious content than other holiday symbols, the city asserted that "the Nativity Scene loses much of its religious meaning in a commercial setting saturated with secularism. The fact is that all of the Christmas symbols have merged and each has become integrated into a single tradition which is dominantly secular."[33]

A Primary Effect That Neither Advances nor Inhibits Religion

The second prong of the Lemon Test is that the principal or primary effect of the alleged violation must neither advance nor inhibit religion. Both sides of the dispute found little significant difference between the "purpose" and "effects" parts of the test. The ACLU position was that the Establishment Clause prohibits government assistance that results in even remote or indirect aid to religion. It was clear to them from the trial that many persons saw the Nativity scene as support for the doctrine of Christianity. Plaintiffs Donnelly and Brown concurred with this view. Most of the letters and phone calls elicited by the suit applauded the city's support for the religious views of the majority. For the plaintiffs the creche had the primary effect of advancing religion.

The city's counterargument was that the existence of religious content in public activities does not necessarily advance religion. It was the defense's position that an important distinction could be made between promoting religion, which is unconstitutional, and acknowledging religion, which is permissible. The context in which a religious symbol is displayed determines whether the religious element constitutes a primary purpose or effect and whether it constitutes an advancement or inhibition of religion.

Pawtucket's Christmas display merely acknowledged the nation's religious heritage while making no attempt to promote a religious message. On the basis of the trial record the city's attorney argued that "it could well be found that the single most important purpose and effect of the display is the commercial promotion of the retail district surrounding Hodgson Park. Any suggestion that the religious promotion of the Nativity Scene represents a primary purpose or effect of the City's Christmas celebration is completely untenable." [34]

Excessive Government Entanglement

The third element of the Lemon Test provides that the disputed activity must not foster excessive government entanglement with religion. From the plaintiffs' perspective the entanglement test addressed two concerns. "First, that government involvement with religion will foster divisiveness which is ultimately detrimental to both government and religion; and secondly, that the government should avoid not only the actual interference and involvement with religion, but also the potential for an appearance of interference with religion." [35]

It was the ACLU's determination that Pawtucket had violated both aspects of the standard. The response of the community to the suit was overwhelming evidence of how symbolically important the Nativity scene was and how religious issues can promote divisiveness. There was little disagreement that most of Pawtucket was outraged over the suit. Plaintiffs concluded that "the City's inclusion of the Nativity Scene in the Christmas display and their vigorous involvement and expression of support for the continued inclusion of such a display, not only fosters divisiveness in the community, but also gives the appearance of interference and involvement with religion on the part of the City." [36]

Defense attorneys vehemently rejected the ACLU's interpretation of entanglement. They argued that the primary purpose of entanglement as interpreted and applied by the Supreme Court was to limit administrative and operational relationships between government officials and private religious groups. *Donnelly v. Lynch* uncovered no such relationships between Pawtucket officials and any such religious group.

Furthermore, the city challenged the view that the public

controversy that resulted from the suit could be used as evidence of divisiveness. "The evidence clearly shows that the Nativity Scene maintained by the City for more than forty years, produced no public controversy whatever until the present action was commenced. As far as public controversy is concerned, virtually all of it arose after the plaintiffs announced their intention to file this law suit and was directed not at the City's forty year maintenance of the Nativity Scene but at the December, 1980 legal challenge to its maintenance."[37] The ACLU contention that the public's response to the practice cannot be separated from its response to the suit was vehemently rejected by the defense.

JUDGE PETTINE DECIDES

On 10 November 1981, nearly eleven months after the suit had been filed, Judge Pettine issued his opinion. In a meticulously drafted seventy-page decision, he ruled that by including a Nativity scene in its Christmas display Pawtucket had violated the Establishment Clause of the First Amendment to the Constitution. To understand the criteria and reasoning he used to resolve the case, it is best that the judge's words speak for themselves.[38]

> The Supreme Court, in one of its major Establishment Clause opinions, noted wearily that "cases arising under the [Religion] Clauses have presented some of the most perplexing questions to come before this Court." The difficult problem is to define "the [elusive] line which separates the secular from the sectarian. . . ."

> I

> Before applying the familiar three-prong test prescribed by the Supreme Court for analysis for Establishment Clause problems, it is necessary to address two arguments made by the City which call into question whether this case presents

an Establishment Clause problem at all. Specifically, the defendants contend first that the erection of the creche has not involved the City in religious activity to any significant degree. They claim that the presence of the creche in the Christmas display merely acknowledges a religious component of an important secular holiday that is celebrated by all Americans. Second, the City also argues that the nativity scene has become largely "secularized" so that its nature or function within the Hodgson Park display is not primarily religious. Each argument is considered in turn.

A. *Christmas as a Secular and Religious Holiday*

Although no case to the Court's knowledge has specifically considered the legitimacy of designating Christmas as a national holiday, the courts that have considered the propriety of governmental participation in various displays and practices connected with Christmas have recognized the obvious fact that Christmas, as celebrated in 20th century America, has a decidedly secular dimension.

This is the Christmas whose central figure is Santa Claus and whose themes are the nontheological ones of goodwill, generosity, peace, and less exaltedly, commercialism. Yet it is equally obvious that for the many 20th century Americans who practice Christianity, there is another Christmas. This is the "original" Christmas whose central figure is Christ, the Son of God, and whose themes are the essentially theological ones of salvation and spiritual peace, renewal, and fulfillment. The City argues that the emergence of a secular dimension to Christmas has rendered the holiday's meaning merely vestigial.

The Court does not agree. Christmas remains a major spiritual feast day for most sects of Christians. It has not lost its religious significance; rather, it has gained a secular significance. Janus-like, it is one holiday with two distinct and very different faces.

If government can, consistent with the Establishment Clause, declare and celebrate Christmas as a national holiday, it is precisely because of this dichotomous nature—that is, because the religious elements of Christmas can be separated out and the secular elements presented more or less in isolation. This is not an uncommon situation in the Establishment Clause area. Recognizing that religion is a real and pervasive component in American life, the Supreme Court has never held that the presence of a religious element in an activity automatically places it beyond the purview of government involvement. As long as there are also strong secular elements, the government may involve itself with the activity *if* it limits itself to promoting only those elements.

A case in point is *Stone v. Graham,* 449 U.S. 39. There the Court held that a Kentucky law that required the posting of a copy of the Ten Commandments on the walls of public school classrooms was constitutionally infirm. Although accepting the possibility that the Ten Commandments could have a place in a properly oriented public school curriculum, the Court refused to accept proffered secular purpose when the state merely posted the Commandments without making any real attempt to distill the secular significance of the Decalogue from its religious elements. Thus, the more dominant and widely recognized the element, the more fastidious must the government be in isolating and emphasizing its concern for only the non-religious elements. Indeed, government has an obligation, if it would not contravene the Establishment Clause, to dissect the secular from the religious even in circumstances where private persons and organizations would perceive and treat the two as an amalgam.

Applying these principles to the case of Christmas, it is this Court's view that a high standard of care is demanded of government when it seeks to "celebrate" this holiday.

The secular and religious dimensions share a common origin and many people, whose holiday observance includes both aspects, may not perceive them clearly demarcated. It is too late in Establishment Clause jurisprudence to suggest that the Government may endorse the Christian view of Christmas as a celebration of the birthday of the Son of God. The fact that a majority of citizens may not consciously draw a line between the Christian and the secular dimensions of Christmas requires that the government be all the more careful to draw a line, and a bright one, between the two, and remain on the clearly secular side.

In the Court's view, this argument is merely a bootstrap. The City relies on the presence of a secular dimension to give the government a toehold and then argues that government, once there on the strength of the secular, has *carte blanche* to enter the allied religious dimension.

The identification of a secular dimension is not a license for government to range throughout the entire field with no thought for the secular or religious character of the area in which it moves. Rather, it is a delimitation of the bounds within which government must remain if it is not to trespass on forbidden ground.

In short, the Court finds that the mere fact that the Christmas holiday has an important secular element does not insulate government involvement in the religious aspects of the holiday from further review under the Establishment Clause.

B. *The Creche as a Religious Symbol*

In contending that it has not violated the Establishment Clause, the City also argues that the inclusion of the creche in the Hodgson Park display is not primarily religious because the nativity scene in essence has become "secularized." As the Court understands this argument, the City

is suggesting that most or all of the religious meaning that
originally inhered in the nativity scene has been lost over
time in the same way that other Christmas symbols, such as
Santa Claus, have shed their religious meaning, or become
"secularized."

The Court finds these comparisons unpersuasive. It is
generally accepted that the concepts of Santa Claus can be
traced to St. Nicholas, a bishop of the early Catholic
Church. However, as one of the plaintiff's witnesses aptly
observed, the modern day Santa Claus owes more to
Clement Moore (and, one suspects, to present day television specials) than to the Fourth Century bishop. Santa
Claus of today is a figure endowed with mythic trappings
having no conceivable connection to his real-world pro-
genitor—he is a jolly bearded figure who lives at the North
Pole and emerges on Christmas Eve in a flying sleigh pulled
by eight reindeer to distribute toys manufactured by elves
by climbing down chimneys. No such drastic mutation can
be found in the case of the nativity scene. The modern day
creche retains its faithfulness to the biblical accounts which
first inspired renderings of what Christians believe took
place at Christ's birth.

Unlike stars, or bells, or trees, the creche is not a common, ordinary object that obtains a religious dimension
only if the viewer understands that it is intended to connote
something more than its facial significance, and possesses
the key to unlock that secondary meaning. The creche is
more immediately connected to the religious importance of
Christmas because it is a direct representation of the full
Biblical account of the birth of Christ. That collection of
figures does not have an everyday meaning that must be
transcended to reach the religious meaning. For anyone
with the most rudimentary knowledge of the religious beliefs and history of Western civilization, the religious mes-

sage of the creche is immediately and unenigmatically conveyed.

In sum, the Court does not understand what meaning the creche, as a symbol, can have other than a religious meaning. It depicts the birth of Christ in a way that is not merely historical. It has not been so altered over the years as to relegate its religious connection to a matter of historical curiosity. It is the embodiment of the Christian view of the birth and nature of Christ. Unless that view has itself lost its religious significance, an artifact that portrays that view simply and unambiguously cannot be other than religious. The City suggests that the creche represents the non-sectarian ethical aspirations of peace and goodwill. Even assuming that this is an independent, secular meaning, the Court finds that it is subordinate to, and indeed flows from the fundamentally religious significance of the creche.

II

The findings that the Christmas holiday has a significant religious aspect and that the creche is a religious symbol do not, of course, resolve the constitutional question. Government may involve itself in activities with a religious content as long as it does so carefully, in ways that avoid the harm that the Establishment Clause was intended to forestall. The Supreme Court has not yet given plenary consideration to a case challenging the use of religious symbolism. Perhaps the closest it has come is the recent case of *Stone v. Graham,* in which the placard of the Ten Commandments posted in Kentucky's public classrooms had some aspect of a religious symbol. Cases involving state aid to religiously-affiliated schools and religious exercises within public schools, although not very helpful on their facts, do provide the basic method of analysis. To pass muster under the Establishment Clause, a statute must have a secular legislative purpose, its principal or primary effect must neither advance nor inhibit religion, and the statute must not foster an excessive government entanglement with religion.

A. *Purpose*

The fundamentals of the purpose test are easily stated. The government action must "reflect a clearly secular . . . purpose." While the rationale offered by the government entity is entitled to deference, the Court must closely scrutinize the stated purpose and ensure that the action was indeed motivated by legitimate secular aims.

In addressing the purpose test, the City first argues that the nativity scene has no purpose that can be considered apart from the purpose of the Hodgson Park display as a whole. In the Court's view, this overstates the role that the context in which the religious component appears plays in the search for purpose.

Although the purpose of the Hodgson Park display as a whole is relevant to the constitutional inquiry, the City may not gloss over the fact that the creche occupies a unique position in the display. Unlike every other element, the nativity scene "appears neither to have been divorced from [its] religious origins nor deprived of [its] centrally religious character by the passage of time." Accordingly, it is necessary to establish why this religious symbol was included with all the secular symbols of Christmas.

In his testimony, Mayor Lynch stated that the purposes for including the creche, like the purposes for the display as a whole, were both economic and cultural or traditional. The first reason can be readily disposed of. The businessmen who testified on behalf of the downtown merchants readily agreed that the creche contributed nothing to the value of the display as a commercial draw.

This leaves the purpose of "culture and tradition." The City argues that the presence of the creche in the display merely acknowledges the religious heritage of the holiday.

The Court is aware that at least two courts, with little hesitation, have accepted as a valid secular purpose for the inclusion of a nativity scene in a public Christmas display the intention to "show how the American people celebrate the holiday season surrounding Christmas." With due respect for the learned judges involved in those decisions, this Court finds that rationale extremely troubling, both in the way it places an apparently neutral, secular characterization on something that may well be far more religious than the label implies, and in the ease with which such a justification can be asserted by the sponsoring government.

Particularly when a belief or practice has been common to the majority for a long time, it becomes easy to regard the belief or practice as a matter of culture or tradition and thereby imply that they have somehow attained a neutral, objective status. "Culture," "religion," "history," "heritage," and "tradition" are not mutually exclusive categories. The values, beliefs, and practices of groups in our society over time become our culture and traditions. However, the fact that a belief is held by sufficient members of society to render it part of our culture as a whole, or that a practice is observed for a sufficient length of time to give it the status of one of our traditions does not mean that the belief or practice ceases to be religious or to be identified with one group.

The Court perceives this danger in characterizing publicly sponsored Christmas displays containing nativity scenes as mere depictions of how the "American people" celebrate the holiday. Even though the majority of the people in our country may be Christian and Christian beliefs and practices by their very pervasiveness have become an important part of our culture and tradition, it must be acknowledged that not every American is a Christian.

The Court is not suggesting that government may never take cognizance of a cultural or traditional element that is religious in character. It *is* suggesting that, in considering the constitutionality of government displays that include a nativity scene, we must at least be frank in recognizing that that part of the display represents "culture" and "tradition" only in the sense that it represents a religious belief held by a substantial segment of our society for a long period of time.

After careful consideration of the circumstances of this case, the Court concludes that the purpose of including a nativity scene in the Hodgson Park display was not merely the neutral recognition that Christmas possesses a religious significance for some people. Rather, Pawtucket's use of a patently religious symbol raises an inference that the City approved and intended to promote the theological message that the symbol conveys.

Although Christians may deplore the growth of the secular dimension and deem it vital to retain the spiritual essence of Christmas as a religious observance of the birth of the Son of God, government may not assist in the fight to keep Christ in Christmas. To do so is to endorse a religious belief and aid in the promulgation of that belief.

B. Effect

To pass Establishment Clause scrutiny, the governmental action must have a "primary effect that neither advances nor inhibits religion." The Supreme Court has recognized that governmental actions may have more than one primary effect. Although governmental activity that confers "some benefit" on religion is not necessarily unconstitutional, the existence of "some legitimate end under the

State's police power" does not necessarily validate such activity. Thus, action having the "direct and immediate effect of advancing religion" violates the First Amendment even though it may immediately and effectively promote legitimate secular ends.

The Supreme Court has stated that the Establishment Clause reaches not only the actual establishment of religion, but also the "*sponsorship,* financial support, and active involvement of the sovereign in religious activity." The government need not overtly support particular sects or rites of worship. If government is "'utilizing the prestige, power, and influence' of a public institution to bring religion into the lives of citizens," the Establishment Clause is violated. Government must be neutral not only in its relations with different sects, but also in its relations with believers and non-believers.

In order for governmental action to pass muster under the Establishment Clause, the government must dispel even the *appearance* of affiliation with the religious message, for apparent sponsorship is as likely as intentional endorsement to breed religious chauvinism in those whose beliefs are seemingly favored as "good" or "true," and alienate those whose beliefs are seemingly dismissed as unworthy of official attention.

Government sponsorship of religious beliefs can occur in ways far more subtle than endowing state churches or mandating acceptance of certain religious rites or tenets. The question is whether, irrespective of the City's purpose, the effect of Pawtucket's "passive" display of a nativity scene as part of its lavish Christmas decorations is the appearance of an official imprimatur on the religious message of the creche and on Christian beliefs, thereby aiding the Christian religion and violating the City's constitutional duty to maintain a neutral position *vis a vis* Christians, non-Christians, and non-believers.

The City suggests that such an effect has not occurred because: 1) prior to this lawsuit, people did not know the City's connection to the Hodgson Park display; 2) the creche represents only a minor and insignificant part of the display; and 3) the creche is only one part of a display consisting primarily of secular Christmas symbols, and the City has made no affirmative attempt to highlight or exploit its religious message. In such circumstances, the City argues, the effect is merely to "acknowledge" the religious heritage and traditions of Christmas without signalling any endorsement of the underlying beliefs.

Having found that the presence of the secular symbols of Christmas does not mute the religious message of the creche, the Court concludes that people who view the Hogdson Park display are not likely to regard the nativity scene as mere "acknowledgement" that religious "heritage" and "traditions" are for some people a part of Christmas.

In view of the creche's unmuted religious message and the undispelled appearance of Pawtucket's affiliation with this message, the Court holds that the City's inclusion of a nativity scene in its Christmas display violates the Establishment Clause. Even if the creche does advance the non-theological goals of peace, charity, and goodwill, the Court finds that the appearance of official sponsorship of Christian beliefs that the creche conveys confers more than a remote and incidental benefit on Christianity. By using a religious symbol in a seasonal celebration of a holiday having a religious significance for some groups, the City has given those groups special status. It has singled out their religious beliefs as worthy of particular attention, thereby implying that these beliefs are true or especially desirable. This aura of governmental approval is a subsidy as real and as valuable as financial assistance. Moreover, Pawtucket's use of the creche encourages in its citizens the belief that the Christian majority has the right to have "its" government reflect and express the religious beliefs that the majority regards as important. Were the notion that it is desirable for government to support the religious views of the majority to become so ingrained as to be accepted without scrutiny and defended without hesitation, a significant breach would be made in the constitutional citadel that protects our religious liberty.

C. Entanglement

The final part of the Establishment Clause tripartite test focuses on the degree and quality of governmental interaction with religion that the challenged activity promotes. The entanglement inquiry has two parts. The first, often referred to as "administrative entanglement," is implicated when the practice at issue brings government officials into close, ongoing contact with the affairs of religious institutions, thereby endangering the independence and integrity of both Church and State.

The second part of the inquiry focuses on "the potential for political divisiveness." This second component assesses the probability that the governmental involvement with religion at issue will encourage division of the polity along religious lines and infect robust political debate with an unhealthy strain of sectarian contentiousness. One need not look back into history to understand the seriousness of this latter concern about political divisiveness; the contemporary situation in several countries amply demonstrates the dreadful struggles and suffering that can result when government becomes a tool for executing religious goals and beliefs.

Unquestionably, administrative entanglement has not occurred in this case. In the Court's opinion, however, Pawtucket's ownership and display of the creche does implicate the political divisiveness strand of the entanglement test.

As the city properly points out, a City-owned creche has been displayed for forty years. Moreover, the practice has been marked by no apparent dissention. That calm history must be acknowledged in assessing the potential for divisiveness in the City's action.

The meaning of this history is ambiguous. Was the silence of the past forty years a healthy sign, indicating that members of minority religions did not feel slighted or alienated by the practice and had no desire for "equal time" for their religious holidays and symbols? Or, was the silence an unhealthy indication of the fear of angering the predominantly Christian majority? In short, was it the product of a pragmatic calculation that enduring one religious symbol celebrating one Christian holiday was a small price to pay for harmony among the townspeople.

The community's reaction to the filing of this lawsuit lends considerable plausibility to the latter interpretation. The City suggests that a "fair representation of the public concern is that it was directed at a perceived attack upon the symbolism of Christmas which is generally viewed as a symbolism of goodwill and brotherhood." However, the Court has found that most of those who communicated their support for the Mayor were not defending a nonsectarian emblem of theologically neutral aspirations. Rather, the creche was championed as the essence of the "true" meaning of Christmas, the vehicle by which belief in and dependence upon God could best be conveyed during the holiday season. Several comments explicitly linked display of the creche with the expression of the majority's faith in Christ and its desire to commemorate his birth, and castigated "minority" attempts to prevent government from reflecting the majority's will in this manner.

In sum, the atmosphere has been a horrifying one of anger, hostility, name calling, and political maneuvering, all prompted by the fact that someone had questioned the City's ownership and display of a religious symbol.

A reasonable interpretation of this public reaction is that Pawtucket's practice of displaying a creche occasions no divisiveness *only* as long as it continues unquestioned. Once challenged, however, the veneer of peace and harmony is stripped away. The absence of religious dissension in Pawtucket over the past forty years does not mean that the governmental action has not produced a division along religious lines. It merely means that until the plaintiffs in this case had the temerity to challenge Pawtucket's official practice, the *potential* for divisiveness remained unrealized. When the challenge finally came, the atmosphere in Pawtucket became charged with religious controversy and polluted by the acrid fumes of religious chauvinism.

The Supreme Court has never held that the potential for political divisiveness is alone sufficient to invalidate a government's action under the Establishment Clause. It has emphasized, however, that this is a "warning signal" that the mandate of the First Amendment has been compromised. Viewing this warning signal of potential divisiveness in conjunction with its earlier findings of improper purpose and impermissible effect, the Court concludes that the Establishment Clause has been violated in this case.

Having spent considerable time exploring what this case is about, the Court feels compelled to add a few words about what it is *not* about. It is not about an infringement of the right of Christians freely to express their belief that Christmas is the day on which the Son of God was born. This decision has nothing to do with the ability of private citizens to display the creche in their homes, yards, businesses, or churches. However, the right to express one's own religious beliefs does not include the right to have one's government express those beliefs simply because the believers constitute a majority.

This Court finds that by including a nativity scene in its Christmas display, the City of Pawtucket has violated the Establishment Clause of the Constitution. Therefore, it is hereby ordered that the City be permanently enjoined from continuing this practice.

So ordered.

III

ROUND TWO: The Court of Appeals

Fine points of law do not compete well with established traditions and with deeply felt religious convictions.

Providence Journal

JUDGES ARE FREQUENTLY ASKED to rule on aspects of constitutional law that most citizens do not appreciate or understand. This is particularly true with issues of individual rights and civil liberties. Although most Americans support Bill of Rights guarantees in the abstract, their level of tolerance for minority rights noticeably decreases when specific cases are applied to general constitutional principles.

Judge Pettine knew that his Nativity ruling would not be a popular one. The decision came just two weeks before the creche was scheduled to be reinstalled in Hodgson Park for the 1981 Christmas season. The intensity of the commitment of heavily Roman Catholic Rhode Island to the religious component of the holiday display was without question. It would be difficult to convince most residents that Pawtucket's forty-year tradition was not in accord with the Constitution. Pettine could only hope that his opinion would serve an educational function that might eventually counterbalance the emotional reaction he anticipated.

If the adverse public reaction to the decision was predictable, the magnitude of the outcry was not. Anger that heretofore had been reserved for the ACLU now turned on Pettine. The opposition came in many forms. Critics of the ruling picketed the federal courthouse with signs that advocated the judge's impeachment. The state's newspapers and Pettine were the recipients of an avalanche of angry mail. "Dear Dis-honorable Judge," one person wrote, "I look forward to your either starting to make your decisions as per the Constitution, or your impeachment from federal court duties." Another said, "I hope Santa Claus puts coal in your stocking, but not enough to heat your home." One woman concluded her letter with, "May the Christ Child forgive you."[1]

Pawtucket officials also condemned the decision. Former mayor Dennis Lynch (who had resigned in July 1981 to become state purchasing agent) called it a "freak," a "Mickey Mouse" decision.[2] Acting mayor William F. Harty said, "I'll never go along with that. We'll have a Nativity scene if I have to play the role of the Christ Child myself."[3] William MacMahon, the city's attorney in the case, accused Pettine of "going contrary to the overwhelming weight of the law."[4]

The Reverend Louis E. Gelineau, Roman Catholic bishop of Providence, stated his opposition to the court's ruling in less emotional terms.

> I grieve that our country, our cities find themselves this Nativity time in legal battles over displays of the religious traditions of our people. Can it be that government is able to represent only the beliefs of secular humanists in our midst? Are judicial pronouncements against the establishment of religion being so rigidly applied that the equally important and equally American exercise of religion is in fact being outlawed? At times it seems that government neutrality is being transformed into government hostility toward a religion.[5]

A puzzling *Pawtucket Times* editorial expressed the view that "legally Judge Pettine is on firm ground and had no choice but to rule the way he did." It concluded, however, that "logically the decision is asinine. . . . With all due respect to Judge Pettine and the Constitution, this is no time to be taking Christ out of Christmas."[6]

A few Protestant clergymen and the *Providence Journal* rallied to the Court's defense. In offering the Pawtucket Congregational Church as a site for the city's creche, minister Paul Howard said, "I don't see why the City has the authority to use the Nativity Scene in a public setting."[7] Bishop George Hunt, leader of the Rhode Island Episcopal Church, expressed the view that Judge Pettine's ruling was "right on target."[8]

Calling the district court ruling "well reasoned, scrupulous in sorting out complex issues, and a solid reinforcement of the constitutional separation of church and state, "a *Journal* editorial seemed to appreciate the decision's educational message.

> The ruling is not likely to be warmly embraced or fully understood. . . . The tendency is strong to polarize for or against, to dismiss the plaintiffs as troublemakers activated by some secret sinister motives. Judge Pettine's finding serves as an important reminder that the public sector is not free to become involved in religious matters without restraint.[9]

PAWTUCKET APPEALS

The first official response from the city was that it would appeal the district court decision to the First Circuit Court of Appeals in Boston. Despite the fact that legal costs to the city were mounting, public sentiment was overwhelmingly supportive of an appeal. Pawtucket risked the chance that if it pursued the case and lost, the ACLU would most likely be able to recover legal fees from the city for its attorneys. However, on the basis that other federal courts had ruled in favor of city-owned Nativity scenes and that only in Rhode Island was the practice outlawed, city officials were confident that they could win at a higher level. Their attorneys petitioned Judge Pettine for a stay of his order banning the creche, pending the appeal.

On the day following the district court decision, ex-mayor Dennis Lynch announced the formation of a private group, Citizens Committed to Continuing Christmas (CCCC). The group was formed to explore the possibility of purchasing the Nativity scene from the city to display it on private property adjacent to the city's display. Solicitation of funds for that purpose brought a generous response from citizens and religious groups.

On 30 November 1981 Judge Pettine refused to delay his order prohibiting the erection of the Nativity scene. The city installed the remainder of the display, leaving the manger scene in storage. On 3 December Mayor Harty announced that he had sold the creche to Lynch's group for three hundred dollars. It was promptly installed in Hodgson Park, in a space left vacant near the city-owned portion of the display. The mayor also reported that the city had requested an immediate stay of the district court order from the first Circuit Court of Appeals in Boston.

Shortly after the creche was installed by Lynch's group, ACLU attorneys asked Judge Pettine to hold Pawtucket in contempt of court. Their complaint alleged that the CCCC's actions gave the appearance of government sponsorship of religion. Pettine rejected the motion and allowed the privately owned creche to remain.

On 11 December 1981 the First Circuit Appeals Court denied Pawtucket's request for a stay of the district court order. It held that because the Nativity scene was currently on display in Hodgson Park, the city could show no irreparable harm. The court also noted that a decision on the city's appeal would be handed down before the scheduled Christmas 1982 erection of the display.

Other Rhode Island communities were also affected by the district court ruling. The pattern of compliance varied. In an effort to abide by the decision, some communities followed Pawtucket's example by enlisting private groups to pay for and erect Nativity displays. In Providence the Knights of Columbus, with the blessings of the mayor, set up a Nativity scene on the steps of City Hall. The contention was that because the display was privately owned, it did not violate Pettine's ruling. The Bristol town administrator vowed to erect the traditional Nativity scene until she got a "specific court order directed to the town of Bristol."[10] The ACLU publicly criticized many of the displays but chose not to initiate any new legal actions until the court of appeals rendered its decision.

THE U.S. COURTS OF APPEALS

The U.S. courts of appeals were created in 1891 as a response to an increasingly unmanageable federal court caseload. They are sometimes referred to as "circuit" courts, harking back to the time when individual Supreme Court justices would "ride circuit" around the country to perform their judicial duties. With the establishment of a new layer of courts in the appeals process, more litigants were afforded an opportunity to carry their cases to a higher court, and the Supreme Court was able to discriminate more carefully which cases it would hear.

The United States is divided geographically into twelve judicial circuits. Each circuit, including one in the District of Columbia, has a court of appeals (see Figure 2).[11] The First Circuit, which heard *Donnelly v. Lynch*, consists of Maine, New Hampshire, Massachusetts, Rhode Island, and Puerto Rico. The court sits for most cases in Boston.

There are presently 156 authorized judgeships for the courts of appeals. The courts range in size from 6 to 28 judges, depending upon the caseload in the circuit. With 6 judges, the First Circuit is the smallest. Like other federal judges, appeals judges are

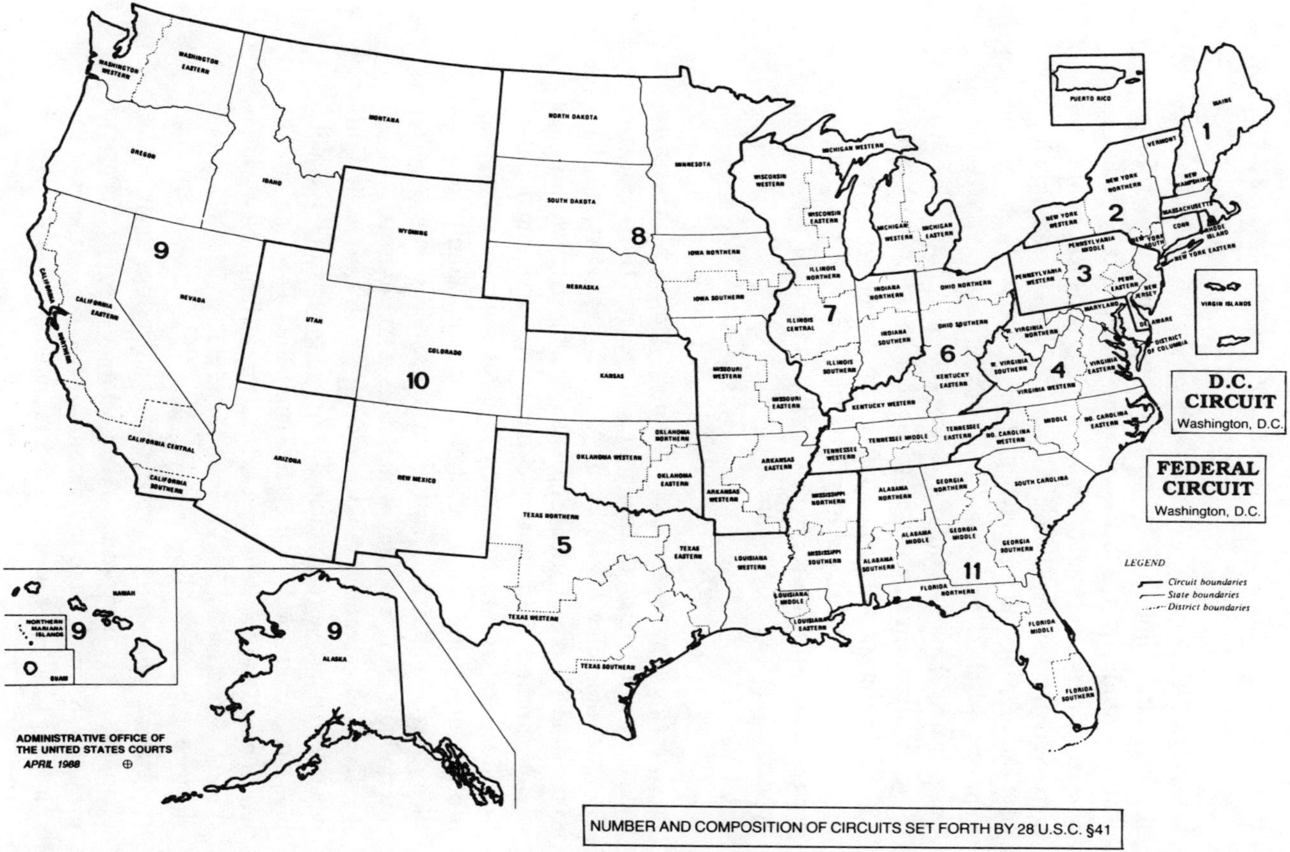

NUMBER AND COMPOSITION OF CIRCUITS SET FORTH BY 28 U.S.C. §41

FIGURE 4. GEOGRAPHICAL BOUNDARIES OF UNITED STATES COURTS OF APPEALS

ADMINISTRATIVE OFFICE OF
THE UNITED STATES COURTS
APRIL 1988

LEGEND

Circuit boundaries
State boundaries
District boundaries

FEDERAL
CIRCUIT
Washington, D.C.

D.C.
CIRCUIT
Washington, D.C.

appointed by the president with the consent of the Senate. Because the circuits include more than a single state in their jurisdiction, the influence of "senatorial courtesy," which profoundly affects the appointment of federal district judges, is substantially reduced. President Reagan eliminated the merit selection commissions that Jimmy Carter had set up, relying instead upon the advice of nine close personal advisors, who constituted his Committee on Federal Judicial Selection.

Because they are the general appellate courts for the federal judicial system, the courts of appeals are "mandatory jurisdiction courts," which means that they are required to hear all of the cases brought before them.[12] Virtually all of their dockets consist of cases originally tried in the district courts within their geographical jurisdiction. Courts of appeals, most notably the District of Columbia circuit court, also hear appeals from administrative rulings of some federal agencies, such as the Federal Communications Commission and the Environmental Protection Agency.

Although over twenty-five thousand new cases are brought to the courts of appeals each year, most district court rulings are neither reviewed nor reversed. In a recent three-year cycle, only one-third of the completed district court cases were taken to the appeals courts.[13] Of these decisions that are pursued, most are either settled prior to an appellate ruling, or reaffirmed by the courts of appeals.

The courts of appeals normally hear cases in three-judge panels. In cases of unusual significance or when the decision of one of its panels is "suspected of error," a court of appeals may sit *en banc,* a situation in which all of the judges of the circuit participate in the case.

To initiate the appeal process a litigant must file a Notice of Appeal petition within thirty days of the district court ruling. Written briefs are submitted. Oral arguments are heard by some courts of appeals, but are dispensed within some circuits, particularly for cases that are considered routine and uncomplicated. No new factual evidence may be presented in the appeal. The major responsibility of the courts of appeals is to review the record of the lower courts in order to determine whether proper procedures have been followed and whether the law has been correctly applied.

Although a court of appeals engages primarily in "error correction," its interpretation of the proper application of a statute often has a significant impact upon the law-making process. Because a variety of interests and perspectives are represented among court of appeals judges, the values supported from circuit to circuit often differ greatly.

The judge senior in length of service on the court who is under sixty-five years of age, and who has not previously served as chief judge, is appointed to serve in that capacity for a seven-year term. In addition a Supreme Court justice is designated to monitor the work of each circuit. The justice's assignment is limited to considering petitions for extraordinary procedures and hearing pleas for stays of execution.

The chief judge, together with the circuit executive (the chief court administrator), selects the panel of judges to hear a case and puts it on the court calendar. Because the workload for the First Circuit was unusually heavy at the time, two local judges were joined by a senior judge from the Seventh Circuit to hear the appeal in *Donnelly v. Lynch*. Senior judges are individuals who have reached sixty-five years of age and who elect not to retire. They may be invited to sit for cases in any of the twelve circuits.

The three judges assigned to the Nativity scene case were

LEVIN H. CAMPBELL, First Circuit. Appointed by President Nixon in 1972. Campbell had previously served on the superior court of Massachusetts and the U.S. district court for Massachusetts. *The Almanac of the Federal Judiciary* evaluated his record as "slightly conservative."[14]

HUGH BOWNES, First Circuit. Appointed by President Carter in 1977. Bownes served as associate judge on the New Hampshire superior court and the United States district court for New Hampshire. The *Almanac* categorizes him as "somewhat liberal."

THOMAS E. FAIRCHILD, senior judge, Seventh Circuit. Appointed by President Johnson in 1966. He previously served on the Supreme Court of Wisconsin. He is categorized as a "LaFollette liberal."

To assist the judges in their preparation for the oral argument of a case, each party is asked to submit a written brief to defend its position. The length, timing, and content format of the briefs are regulated by federal rules of appellate procedure. In *Donnelly v. Lynch* the briefs repeated much of the argument presented to the district court. An outline of the plaintiff and defense briefs is included in Figure 3.

The panel of judges heard oral argument on the case on 7 April 1982. Attorneys for both sides were allotted fifteen minutes each to summarize their arguments. At the conclusion of testimony and questioning from the panel, the judges retired to discuss the issues and reach their decision.

THE COURT OF APPEALS DECIDES

On 3 November 1982, in a 2–1 split decision, the court of appeals affirmed the district court ruling. The majority opinion was authored by Judge Fairchild. After reaffirming the plaintiff's standing to sue, Fairchild argued that Judge Pettine had correctly ruled that the Nativity scene retained its fundamentally religious significance, and that Christmas remains a major spiritual feast day for most Christians. The major question for the court was whether the lower court had correctly applied Supreme Court precedent to the case. Judge Fairchild considered *Donnelly v. Lynch* in light of Supreme Court establishment de-

FIGURE 3. SUMMARY OF PLAINTIFF AND DEFENSE BRIEFS TO U.S.
COURT OF APPEALS

I. The Plaintiffs argued that the district court ruling should be affirmed because

   1. The trial court judge's determination that Christmas has retained its religious significance and that the Nativity scene represents a religious statement concerning the birth and nature of Jesus Christ was correct.

   2. The district court correctly applied the Lemon Test standard in finding that

      (a) The Nativity scene was included in the display to express the city's approval and endorsement of the religious message it conveys.

      (b) The appearance of official sponsorship of Christian belief that the creche conveyed conferred more than a remote and incidental benefit on Christianity.

      (c) The potential for political divisiveness engendered by the city's actions was a "warning signal" that the Establishment Clause had been compromised.

II. The defense argued that the district court decision should be reversed because

   1. The city's sponsorship of a Christmas display that included a Nativity scene did not violate the Establishment Clause because the display was dominantly secular in content and impact.

   2. Where the primary purpose and effect of a secular Christmas display does not advance or inhibit religion, a creche that is an integrated component of the display also does not have a primary purpose or effect advancing or inhibiting religion.

   3. The subjective impression of a "tiny handful" of miscellaneously selected members of the general public that the Nativity scene advanced a specific religious message was not sufficient to reach a violation of the Establishment Clause.

   4. Public controversies that resulted from the ACLU lawsuit were not sufficient evidence to substantiate "divisiveness" creating "excessive governmental entanglement."

cisions, noting that a new decision that came down after Pettine's ruling was relevant to the case.[15]

Judge Fairchild wrote:

> Subsequent to both the decision by the district court and oral argument in this court, the Supreme Court decided in *Larson v. Valente*, 456 U.S. 228, that: "the *Lemon v. Kurtzman* 'tests' are intended to apply to laws affording a uniform benefit to all religions, and not to provisions . . . that discriminate among religions." To statutes, such as the one before it, effectively granting a denominational preference, the Court found appropriate a test of "strict scrutiny," which requires invalidation unless the provision in question "is justified by a compelling governmental interest." Because the City's ownership and use of the Nativity scene is an act which discriminates between Christian and non-Christian religions, it must be evaluated under the test of "strict scrutiny."

> Specifically, the district court found that defendants, after fair opportunity to do so, were unable to advance any legitimate secular purpose for inclusion of the creche in the outdoor display, and that by such action the City in fact had "tried to endorse and promulgate religious beliefs." We find no error in this part of the district court's analysis. That being so, it follows inexorably that defendants established no compelling governmental interest in erection of the Nativity scene. If one is unable to demonstrate any legitimate purpose or interest, it is hardly necessary to inquire whether a compelling purpose or interest can be shown.

> We note that our result is consistent with the district court's finding—with which we agree—that erection of the creche had a primary effect of advancing religion and therefore was unconstitutional. However, we are unwilling to place much weight on the court's determination that the

City's actions risked political divisiveness along religious lines. As the court noted, this factor alone has never been held sufficient to invalidate governmental action, and First Amendment scholars have questioned and criticized the political divisiveness strand of the entanglement test on historical and prudential grounds.

Finally, we are aware that our decision is apparently at odds with a recent decision of the United States District Court of Colorado. In *Citizens Concerned for Separation of Church and State v. City and County of Denver,* that court expressly declined to follow the district court opinion in the present case and held that the erection of a Nativity scene as part of the City and County of Denver's annual Christmas lighting display did not violate the Establishment Clause. We think it sufficient to note that we have considered the reasoning in *Citizens Concerned* and to the extent it is legally inconsistent with the present decision, find it unpersuasive.

In a concurring opinion, Judge Bownes developed both the secular and religious historical roots of Christmas, concluding that

> Christmas has roots that are embedded deeply in the Christian religion; its roots also extend to folk customs and pagan rites that predate the birth of Christ. The creche, however, is tied firmly to the Christian religion; it tells the story of the birth of Christ, the Son of God. Unlike today's Christmas holiday, the creche is not the result of the combination of folk culture and tradition. The creche is purely a religious symbol; this is the distinction between the creche and Christmas as a holiday. It is a distinction of constitutional significance. Although the government may recognize Christmas as a holiday and even participate in some of its secular traditions, it may not participate in the Christian celebration of Christmas. To view the creche as only one of

the many symbols of the Christmas holiday season is to denigrate its religious significance and misinterpret the historical background of Christmas.

Judge Campbell dissented, arguing, in part:

I think the court errs in holding that the display in a public park during the Christmas season of characters and animals associated with the scene constitutes "an establishment of religion" within the First Amendment. Unassociated, as they were, with the performance of any religious rites, the figures did not "establish" religion in the context in which they were presented. They simply contributed to the message that the holiday they represented was at hand.

It must be borne in mind that this creche was but part of a larger display. . . . The whole melange, including the creche, was nothing more than a potpourri of well-recognized Christmas symbols. Had a solitary creche been displayed in July, one might see it as designed to serve chiefly religious ends, since there would then be no holiday with which it was particularly identified. But creches and Santas in December are as typically symbolic of Christmas as turkeys and Pilgrims in November are symbolic of Thanksgiving.

The fact is, Christmas, with its clear religious as well as its secular roots, has become an ingrained part of our culture. Were one today to seek to make a national holiday out of such a church festival, constitutional objections might well prevail. But Christmas is water over the dam. And so, I would argue, are all its established symbols, including carols and creches. To retain the holiday but outlawing these ancient symbols seems to me an empty and even rather boorish gesture.

One significance of the appeals court's opinion is in its application of "strict scrutiny" to the Nativity scene question. The result is a much more rigorous test to sustain government activity than is required by the *Lemon* standards. Under Judge Fairchild's interpretation of *Larson,* only if Pawtucket could demonstrate a "compelling governmental interest" could the creche be displayed. How often would government's efforts to accommodate religion reach the stage of a "compelling interest?" If strict scrutiny became the accepted standard in establishment cases, the wall of separation between church and state would be much more difficult to penetrate.

It is also interesting to note that each of the judges voted according to the "ideological leanings" reported by the *Almanac of the Federal Judiciary.* Fairchild and Bownes supported a liberal interpretation of the First Amendment that the rights of the minority were paramount. Judge Campbell relied on a conservative view that the longstanding tradition of the Nativity scene in Pawtucket was "water over the dam." This is a reminder of Levy's suggestion that, notwithstanding the tests the courts have evolved to operationalize establishment principles, the determining factor in the decision-making process often turns out to be the perspectives of the individual judges that hide behind the prevailing tests.

Because few cases are appealed from the courts of appeals to the Supreme Court, and the Supreme Court turns down most petititons for review, the great majority of appeals court decisions are left intact.[16] However, the ruling in *Donnelly v. Lynch* was of the type to suggest it was a prime candidate for review. First, the opinion was a divided one. A dissenting opinion encourages the losing side to pursue its claim to a higher court. Second, the decision contradicted other lower court decisions. Most important, the lower court rulings demonstrated that establishment law was very unsettled. Two federal courts had used different criteria to reach the same result. The confusion would need to be clarified.

Meanwhile, in Rhode Island publicly sponsored Christmas

displays became a matter of controversy for a third holiday season. Religious leaders disagreed over whether privately owned manger scenes displayed on public property were constitutional. The ACLU continued to advance the view that Pawtucket's display "created the obvious appearance of government sponsorship." In response to the recurring unrest, the *Providence Journal* asked, "Wouldn't it be nice if Christmas could come and go without annual attempts by well meaning public officials to shove it down people's throats?"[17]

On 3 November 1982 Mayor Henry S. Kinch, the third Pawtucket chief executive to become embroiled in the controversy, announced that the city would ask the Supreme Court to overturn the appeals court decision. Taking many of his cues from Judge Campbell's appeals court dissent, the mayor reiterated the city position. "We continue to believe that a 40–year tradition in this City in no way violates the First Amendment of the U.S. Constitution."[18]

If it agreed to hear the case, the Supreme Court would be the last court to have the opportunity to substantiate Pawtucket's claim.

IV

A FINAL HEARING:
The Supreme Court

It is emphatically the province and duty of the judicial department to say what the law is.

> Chief Justice John Marshall
> *Marbury v. Madison,* 1803

A VISITOR TO THE SUPREME COURT cannot mistake the influence of John Marshall upon American constitutional law. On entering the building one is immediately drawn to the larger-than-life statue of our third chief justice, which dominates the main lobby. Behind him, etched in marble, are the brightly illuminated words which begin this chapter. If architecture, inscriptions, portraits, statues, and the majesty of the "Marble Palace" are indicative of the respect in which the Supreme Court is held and the influence it exerts on the American political system today, no one would challenge Marshall's bold claim of power for the judiciary.

The Supreme Court has not always played the central role in government that it does today. Article III of the Constitution, which defines the power of the judiciary, was not nearly as specific or precise as the corresponding articles outlining legislative and executive power. It was left primarily to the Court itself to give specific meaning to the Framers' general guidelines. Beginning with *Marbury v. Madison* in 1803, when John Marshall claimed for judges the power of judicial review, and extending throughout the history of the Court, the justices' decisions have elaborated upon and fine-tuned their role as the final arbiter of the constitutionality of the actions of Congress, of the Chief Executive, and of state governments. By the mid-twentieth century, Justice Felix Frankfurter could confidently claim, "The Supreme Court is the Constitution."

Although constitutional scholars continue to debate the intention of the Framers for the judiciary, and the proper role of the courts in the political system, few, if any, would deny the need for an agency of government to enforce constitutional limitations. In a government of divided power, disputes over constitutional authority among the branches of the national government and between the national government and the states are unavoidable. The interests of the majority will inevitably clash with the rights of the minority. Judges, by virtue of their lifetime appointments, are more likely to be "disinterested" and "neutral" in their actions. Courts provide a buffer to mitigate the effects of pressures exerted by other political institutions and by public opinion when they do not conform to the settled doctrine of the Constitution.

Does a practice that allows nine "unelected" justices to resolve constitutional disputes conform to the requirements of a democratic political system? One student of the Court commented upon the democratic nature of judicial review in the following manner:

> If the Constitution is in reality a democratic document—made so by usage and acceptance—then one may assume that the institutions set up for the Constitution are also democratized by long acceptance. . . . Judicial review is democratically sanctioned by virtue of the acquiescence of

the public. . . . The Supreme Court is democratic not in the representative sense but in the sense that it was created by the will of the people and is performing a function sanctioned by the same will.

It is necessary to draw a distinction between the will of the people as expressed in a constitution and that will as expressed in an act of the legislature. If there is a conflict, the higher will must rule—unless the Constitution itself is to be changed. The very fact that the Supreme Court is not an elective body makes it more democratic; for it is the one part of our government that is in a practical position to insulate itself against the current (legislative) public opinion as opposed to the more permanent (constitutional) opinion.[1]

If the power of the Supreme Court is great, so too are its limits. The Court must function in a political environment replete with an extensive system of checks and balances. Judges can decide only those cases that grow out of actual disputes; they cannot reach out to solve problems on their own. The Court has no power to enforce its decisions; it depends on the other parts of the system to abide by its rulings. The Constitution gives Congress the power to impeach judges, to alter the structure of the federal courts, and to manipulate their agenda by removing certain areas of law from their jurisdiction. Legislation may be passed to evade a Court ruling, and a constitutional amendment may be enacted to overrule a Court decision.

The Court also recognizes its limited role by self-imposed restraints. The "presumption of constitutionality" requires that the burden of proof in a case be on the challenger to government actions; any doubts are resolved in favor of the government. Adherence to the "rule of precedent" demands that the Court give considerable weight to previous decisions in settling disputes. The "doctrine of political questions" means that some questions are more properly decided by the "political" branches of the government. Highly controversial questions are often postponed until public passions have subsided. Finally, judges are aware that "they are all-powerful as long as the people respect the law but they would be impotent against popular neglect or contempt of the law."[2] A Court that abuses its independence by consistently ignoring strong currents of public opinion will discover that its political legitimacy and vital public support may be eroded.

Life on the Supreme Court is made more interesting by virtue of the fact that not all justices have the same understanding of its role. Advocates of "judicial restraint" believe that judges should interpret the Constitution in the literal sense that the Founding Fathers wrote it. "Self-restrainers" will give the benefit of the doubt to the political branches of government unless they see a clearly obvious violation of the Constitution. Proponents of "judicial activism," on the other hand, argue that it is the responsibility of the Court to adapt its rulings to reflect current conditions and philosophies about the role of government. More inclined to say "no" to government, activist judges are often accused of usurping the "policy-making" role of elected officials.

These clashing philosophies are related to political ideology, a factor that is often important in the naming of new justices. Franklin Roosevelt's famous court-packing plan in the late 1930s was stimulated by his belief that the Court's conservative economic views were out of step with the times. As a reaction to the liberal "activist" Court of Chief Justice Earl Warren (1954–1969), recent Republican presidents have recruited conservative "restraint"-oriented jurists to alter the Court's ideological balance. In 1987 Ronald Reagan's difficulty in finding a successor to Justice Lewis F. Powell who was acceptable to the U.S. Senate was in large part a dispute over ideology. Competing conceptions of the Court's role have structured the debate about the proper balance between government authority and individual rights, the question with which *Lynch v. Donnelly* deals. This topic is addressed more specifically in the concluding chapter.

Chief Justice William H. Rehnquist described the work of the Supreme Court as consisting of essentially three different functions. First, it must choose from among the more than 4,000 appeal requests each year, somewhere around 150 cases that it will consider. Second, the Court decides these cases, and that includes studying the briefs, hearing oral arguments by the lawyers for the parties, and voting on them at conference. Finally, the justices prepare written opinions supporting the result reached by the majority and separate opinions and dissenting opinions by those justices who do not agree with the reasoning of the majority.[3] The most difficult hurdle for a party seeking a Supreme Court reconsideration of a lower court decision, however, is in persuading the Court that the case is important enough to be included on the Court's limited and very selective docket.

APPLYING FOR CERTIORARI

The Supreme Court possesses both original and appellate jurisdiction. As a matter of practice, however, virtually all of the cases it hears come to it on appeal and are self-selected by the justices. Although Article III of the Constitution provides that the Court will have original jurisdiction "in all Cases affecting Ambassadors, other public Ministers and Consuls, and those in which a State shall be a party," grants of concurrent jurisdiction to other courts now limit the Court's original jurisdiction to cases involving two or more states.[4]

The pressures of a steadily increasing number of cases has led to a recurring concern about the Court's ability to handle its heavy volume of cases satisfactorily. In 1891 the creation of the federal courts of appeals provided temporary relief. When the situation worsened again, Congress passed what is commonly called the Certiorari Act of 1925. The legislation provided that in the majority of cases there would be no automatic right of appeal to the Supreme Court. The review of lower court decisions would be at the discretion of the justices.

In most instances the party that seeks to overturn a lower court decision must apply for Supreme Court consideration through a petition for certiorari. The petition is a statement that identifies the constitutional question presented by a case and argues why the Supreme Court should reverse the lower court judgment. The Court follows a practice that the votes of four of the nine justices are required for a case to be accepted (the "rule of four").

Although the Certiorari Act substantially increased the Court's ability to manage its workload, it did nothing to stem the increasing number of appeals requests. Over the past forty years the average number of petitions filed has increased by over 300 percent; the number of cases decided, however, has not increased proportionately. During the 1983–1984 term, when *Lynch v. Donnelly* was argued, 4,218 petitions for certiorari were filed, but only 162 signed opinions were issued.

Some observers point out that the Court's response to the massive growth in certiorari petitions has been to tighten its standards for acceptance, with the result that important cases go unheard. To alleviate this situation, former chief justice Warren Burger, who once assessed the problem as "approaching a disaster area," joined others in advocating that a national court of appeals be created to take on some of the Court's work.

Chief Justice Rehnquist acknowledges that the Court is sometimes "stretched quite thin" and that it must "turn down many [cases] that several justices . . . think do meet the standard for review."[5] He places considerable faith, however, in the quality of the judicial process in the lower courts. He accepts the view that the Supreme Court's role today is not to guarantee that justice is done to every litigant, but to adjudicate issues of public policy where the result has a significant influence beyond its effect on the individual parties to a case. The individual litigant becomes an illustrative figure rather than a principle actor in settling major questions of constitutional interpretation.

The number of cases that the Supreme Court can accept in a given year is a function of the time available to the nine justices. The Court is in session from 1 October to 30 June. For a two-week period at the beginning of the term, the justices sit as a body to hear oral arguments on cases that have been accepted. Normally twenty-four cases are considered during this time bloc. In addition the judges meet privately in conference during this period to consider new certiorari petitions and to discuss and vote on those cases that have been recently argued. (See Table 2.) The Court then recesses for two weeks to allow justices time to write their opinions and to prepare for the cases that will be argued in the next two-week period. This four-week cycle is repeated seven times during the term.[6] The summer months are used to complete unfinished work and to prepare for the next

TABLE 2. SUPREME COURT CALENDAR WORK CYCLE

	Mon.	Tues.	Wed.	Thurs.	Fri.
Weeks 1 and 2	Oral arg.	Oral arg.	Oral arg.		Conference to
A.M.	[2 cases]	[2 cases]	[2 cases]	Study time	consider cases argued Tues. and
P.M.	Oral arg. [2 cases]	Oral arg. [2 cases]	Oral arg. [2 cases] + conference to decide cases argued Mon.		Wed. and to decide certiorari petitions
Weeks 3 and 4	Court is in recess to write opinions, study briefs of forthcoming cases, and consider certiorari requests				

term. In recent years the justices have begun meeting during the last week of September to dispose of certiorari petitions that have accumulated during the summer recess.

Petitions for certiorari are examined initially by the justices' law clerks. Justices are entitled to select four recent law school graduates to assist them with their work. Clerks generally serve one-year terms. Recently the majority of the justices have pooled their law clerks in order to streamline the consideration of petitions for certiorari.[7] The "cert pool," as it has come to be called, writes the initial memos outlining the facts and arguments of each petition. Justices commonly ask their clerks to review the memoranda to identify those cases that have unusual merit. Some Court observers question whether a reliance on law clerks to perform the screening function is an abandonment of the justices' responsibilities. The counterargument to this criticism is that the criteria for reviewing petitions is standardized and that with nine justices' offices monitoring the process, the chance that an important case will escape the attention of the justices is not very great.

The Supreme Court has three options in its consideration of a certiorari petition. It can reject the petition altogether, which has the effect of leaving the lower court decision in place. It can review a case for an immediate decision, which is usually accompanied by a brief *per curiam* (unsigned) opinion. Or it can accept the case for full consideration.

A number of factors influence the Court's decision whether to grant certiorari. A case that is accepted will almost always have broad public significance and raise a constitutional issue that has been actively litigated in the lower courts. If there is a conflict of opinion in the lower courts or if a lower court decision appears to conflict with an earlier Supreme Court decision, the justices may want to clarify the law. If the lower court's reasoning departs significantly from the "accepted interpretation" of the law or if a controversy involves the interpretation of a statute never before construed by the court, four justices may be persuaded to put the case on the Court's agenda. The important point is that because the Court accepts less than one in twenty-five cases it is asked to hear, it limits its docket to ones involving important questions of public policy that transcend the interests of the parties involved.

On 26 January 1983, attorneys for Pawtucket filed a petition for a writ of certiorari in *Lynch v. Donnelly*.[8] (Because the court of appeals sustained the ACLU claim, the names in the cases are now reversed. Pawtucket, through former mayor Dennis Lynch, becomes the petitioner, and the ACLU, through Donnelly, is the respondent in the case.) The petition was carefully crafted to persuade the Court to accept the case. The city emphasized that the lower court rulings in the suit were in conflict with other federal court decisions and with decisions of state courts of last resort. The case also raised an important question of constitutional interpretation that had not previously been considered by the Supreme Court.

Specifically, petitioners argued that the court of appeals ruling misinterpreted the "spirit" of the Court's establishment decisions. When it concluded that "Christmas could only be recognized by government if its religious components were 'separated out' from the secular elements of the holiday, the city alleged that the court of appeals ignored the fact that "the existence of and legitimacy of religious tradition in American institutions and American culture has long been recognized by this Court. The constitutional bar against public promotion of religion has consistently preserved the permissibility of neutral acknowledgement of those religious roots which exist in American culture."

Encouraged by Judge Campbell's appeals court dissent and decisions of other state and federal courts, the petitioners emphasized the city's position that the "context" of the display was of unusual importance to the case.

It is respectfully submitted that on the record in this case the creche has no purpose or effect at all apart from its

surroundings. In applying the tri-partite test to a government activity which contains a religious element, the appropriate focus is not on the religious element but on the
activity of which it is a part. The question presented in this
case is whether the Establishment Clause requires government in its activities aggressively to root out from its cultural observance all vestiges of the well recognized religious
traditions of the American people. . . . The Court of Appeals in this case should have applied the tri-partite test not
to the creche but rather to the City's Christmas celebration.

The petitioners found an additional support for granting
certiorari in the case by virtue of the court of appeals' application of *Larson v. Valente*. The effect of applying a standard of
"strict scrutiny" approach to establishment cases "would be to
supplant the tri-partite test of *Lemon*. If the existence of a religious incident in public activities is automatically suspect and
subject to 'strict scrutiny' the *Lemon* test analysis is inappropriate and Establishment Clause doctrine has undergone fundamental revision."

Conflict in the lower court, lack of a specific Supreme Court
ruling on the Nativity scene question, and legal reasoning that
appeared to contradict prevailing establishment standards persuaded Pawtucket's attorneys that *Lynch v. Donnelly* was a case
for which certiorari should and would be granted.

Attorneys for the ACLU filed a brief in opposition to the petition for certiorari in which they argued that Pawtucket was
steering the Court away from the major constitutional question
raised by the case.[9] In seeking a review of the constitutionality of
an entire Christmas display, the ACLU alleged that the city had
misconstrued and altered the scope of the lower court decisions.
For the respondents the proper characterization of the issue and
scope of the review was simply, "Did the lower courts correctly
determine that a municipality's ownership, erection, and display

of a Nativity scene depicting the Biblical story of the birth of Jesus Christ violate the Establishment Clause of the First Amendment to the United States Constitution, made applicable to the states by the Fourteenth Amendment?"

Respondents argued that certiorari should be denied because both the district court and court of appeals decisions were in complete accord with the relevant decisions of the Supreme Court. The appearance of conflict in the lower courts was "illusory." Clarification of the appeals court reliance on *Larson* was unwarranted because the majority opinion also agreed that the city had violated both the purpose and effects tests set forth in *Lemon*. Even if the introduction of "strict scrutiny" were misplaced, the decision would remain the same, unless the Supreme Court also disagreed with its application and interpretation of *Lemon v. Kurtzman*.

On 18 April 1983 the clerk of the Supreme Court unceremoniously reported that the justices had agreed in conference to put *Lynch v. Donnelly* on its docket of cases. Votes on certiorari petitions and the reasoning for accepting or refusing to consider a case are not announced in court.

Within weeks after it had agreed to hear the Nativity scene case, the Supreme Court issued two establishment rulings that gave comfort to Pawtucket and its supporters. In *Mueller v. Allen,* the Court in a 5−4 decision lowered the "wall of separation" by ruling that a state, through tax deductions, could provide financial aid to parents who send their children to parochial schools.[10] As long as the deduction was available to all parents with children in school, whether the school was private, parochial, or public, any advantage to religion was incidental to the predominantly secular purpose of insuring a well-educated citizenry.

Potentially more important for proponents of publicly supported Nativity scenes was *Marsh v. Chambers.*[11] In a 6−3 decision, the Court permitted state funding of a chaplain and the recitation of prayers in the Nebraska legislature. The case was important because the Court did not utilize the three-part Lemon Test. Instead it argued that the practice was constitutional because of its longstanding acceptance at the federal and state levels throughout history. If "historical acceptance" was sufficient to justify government accommodation of religion, the attorneys in the Nativity scene dispute had a new line of judicial reasoning to consider in their written briefs to the Court.

TO BRIEF THE COURT

Six months elapsed between the grant of certiorari in *Lynch v. Donnelly* and the next formal stage in the process, oral argument. During this time written briefs were filed with the Court by both parties. Other individuals, organizations, and governmental agencies who had an interest in the case also petitioned the Court for permission to submit amicus curiae briefs. The consent of both parties in a case, or one party and the Court, is required for permission to be granted. Although they are not directly involved in the litigation, these "friends of the Court" often emphasize information or interpretations of a point of law that the major litigants may not have raised. Amicus briefs also provide interest groups with their only way to "lobby" the courts.

The Nativity scene also raised an important concern for part of the Reagan administration's "social issues" agenda, the effort to promote religion in American life. More than other presidents, Reagan encouraged the Department of Justice to file "friend of the Court" briefs for important Court cases. Solicitor General Rex E. Lee, the government's lawyer "at the bar of the Court," requested and was granted permission to present the administration's position on publicly supported Nativity scenes.

After it had successfully bucked the one to twenty-five odds that a case will be accepted by the Court, *Lynch v. Donnelly* attracted increasing interest from the national media. The *New*

York Times welcomed the opportunity to define the boundary between church and state. Even before the High Court's consideration of the issue, the paper editorialized that "Courts cannot allow a government to buy and install Christian symbols and inflict them on non-Christians or nonbelievers."[12] The case also occasioned the visit of Phil Donahue to Providence for a debate between the parties on his nationally televised talk show. What Donahue feared might be a "boring program" turned into a heated discussion that also helped to raise the issue from a local matter to a national concern.

Several weeks before an oral argument is to occur, briefs are filed by the parties to the case and "friends." Court rules prescribe that the statements of the petitioner (Pawtucket) and the respondent (ACLU) be limited to fifty pages each. *Amicus* briefs must not exceed thirty pages. Pawtucket was supported in *Lynch* by "friends'" briefs on behalf of the United States (solicitor general) and four nonprofit private organizations (the Coalition for Religious Liberty, the Freedom Council, the Legal Foundation of America, and the Washington Legal Foundation). The ACLU position was supplemented by statements from the Anti-Defamation League of B'nai B'rith, the American Jewish Congress, the American Jewish Committee, and the National Council of the Churches of Christ. The following summaries of the written statements emphasize those portions of the arguments that had not been raised in the lower courts.

Petitioner and "Friends"

Pawtucket submitted a petitioner's brief on 10 June 1983. The city also responded to the ACLU's statement with a "reply brief" dated 15 September 1983.[13] The second statement permitted the city's attorney to integrate into his argument the Supreme Court's decision in *Marsh v. Chambers* (decided 5 July 1983), which sustained the Nebraska legislature's practice of opening its sessions with a prayer offered by a chaplain salaried by the state. Attorney William MacMahon directed the justices' thoughts toward the particular setting of the city's display.

The removal of all religiosity from government activity is neither practical nor desirable because the religious tradition of the American people is too deeply ingrained in the life of the nation. Religious origins in American culture do not prohibit public observance of contemporary secular events which derive from those religious origins. Where the secular aspects of an activity dominate the religious aspects, a government may engage in such activity without offending the Establishment Clause.

The American Christmas is a secular national folk festival which derives from the Christian celebration of the nativity. The nativity theme has been heavily overshadowed by the secular components of the national festival. The contemporary festival is a vast conglomeration of folk customs and symbols, feasting and fraternizing, music, literature, and art. The religious origins in the holiday have evolved into secular humanism and the nativity scene has evolved into a major element of the artistic component of the national festival.

The issue in this case is whether the City's celebration of Christmas is a dominantly religious or a dominantly secular activity. The City is no more sponsoring a creche than it is sponsoring a snowman, a Christmas tree, or a Santa Claus; it is sponsoring all of these and much more as part of an integrated celebration of a legitimate national holiday. If the sponsorship of the creche were to be invalid under the *Lemon* tri-partite test, it could only be so because the creche makes the entire celebration a religious activity.

The City's Christmas celebration does not violate the *Lemon* test. The government action has a secular purpose of joining with the community in celebrating the national legal symbol of Christmas. The passive inclusion of those symbols, both secular and sectarian, which are traditionally associated with the American folk festival of Christmas, does not result in the advancement or inhibition of religion. Since the government activity is secular and since it does not conduct that activity in affiliation with any outside religious group, its Christmas celebration does not involve entanglement with religion.

In *Marsh* this Court reaffirmed the long standing principle that the mere recognition of religion by government is not a promotion of its content. What the Founding Fathers sought to prohibit in the First Amendment was "proselytizing activity." The ACLU position is that any governmental display of "undeniably sectarian" material is a violation of the Establishment Clause. Acceptance of this position would mean that a finding of explicitly religious content in government activity compels a conclusion of unconstitutionality. This argument is in sharp conflict with the decisions of the Court. It is not the explicitly religious nature of the material but rather the manner in which it is presented which determines whether government is promoting its religious content or merely recognizing religious traditions.

Solictor General Lee argued for the United States that Pawtucket's display should be permitted on the basis of the historical position of religion in American culture and traditions.[14]

The United States has a substantial interest in this case, which raises the question whether the Constitution requires a rigid and artificial exclusion from our public ceremonies and celebrations of all acknowledgement of the religious elements in our national traditions. The federal government has, from the earliest days of the Republic to the present, felt free to acknowledge and recognize that religion is a part of our heritage and should continue to be a part of our public life.

Our submission is that it was not the purpose of the Framers of the Constitution to require government wholly and rigidly to exclude religion from our public occasions. Both before and after the drafting and enactment of the Establishment Clause, governmental acknowledgement of a Supreme Being was a naturally accepted feature of American public life. Government officials invoked the name of God, asked His blessings upon our Nation, and encouraged our people to do the same.

Today, as in the earliest days of the Republic the government continues to recognize that our Nation's heritage includes a religious element. Coins have borne the legend "In God We Trust" since 1865 and this phrase was made the national motto in 1956. Many patriotic songs similarly acknowledge our dependence upon God and invoke His blessings. Presidential proclamations and messages continue to mark Thanksgiving as a day of prayer.

The familiar three-part test also seems inapposite and artificial here—although the petitioners' brief shows that Pawtucket's practice does meet that test. The traditional religious references and reminders that fill American life should not depend, for their validity, on the dubious assertion that they are wholly perfunctory and meaningless. It was never the purpose of the Framers to secularize our public life so rigidly that we cannot continue to mark our public holidays in a manner that includes traditional acknowledgment of their religious character.

Amicus briefs for the four private organizations that supported Pawtucket's position argued against the "strict scrutiny" standard that had been applied to the case by the court of appeals. The major thrust of their arguments is summarized.[15]

The First Circuit Court of Appeals was incorrect in applying a strict scrutiny analysis to determine whether the inclusion of the creche was constitutional. The Framers would have been appalled that the First Amendment could be utilized to prohibit the practice. The rule of separation that the Framers had in mind when they drafted the First Amendment was to be implemented in a climate of accommodation and benevolence, not of hostility toward religion. To affirm the First Circuit's ruling would be to sanction hostility to the religious heritage of our nation and disaffirm the principle of benevolent neutrality.

The Court below would outlaw official "display" of an ancient symbol depicting the historical and religious roots of the Christmas holiday, but would permit official "observance of the holiday itself, named for and commemorating the birth of Jesus Christ. The logic is not only specious, it produces an absurd result. The transformation of the holiday would involve government in a misleading, even dishonest act and thereby demean the institutions of government itself. It would interfere directly in the task of religious institutions, since it would give apparent government approval to the replacement of their interpretation of Christmas with the exaltation of the secular. And it would threaten and insult those who celebrate Christmas as a religious holiday by an official denial of the aspects they cherish most.

The ACLU and "Amici"

On 18 August 1983 Attorney Amato DeLuca filed the brief of the respondents with the Court.[16] Assisting in the preparation of the brief were attorneys representing the national office of the ACLU. The argument was advanced that prior court establishment decisions weighed heavily on the side of the ACLU in this case, and that the reliance of Pawtucket and the solicitor general on the reasoning in the legislative chaplaincy case (*Marsh*) was misplaced.

Petitioners purchase and display of the Nativity scene—paid for with public funds and given official government support—violates the Establishment Clause in three fundamental ways: (1) by placing the imprimatur on the state on religious beliefs; (2) by discriminating among religious beliefs; and, most basically, (3) by failing to satisfy any, much less all, of the three purpose, effect, and entanglement tests used to determine the permissibility of government activity which assists religion.

The Nativity scene, which symbolically re-enacts a central event in Christian religious belief, is undeniably sectarian. In *Stone v. Graham* the Court held that "the mere posting" of the undeniably sectarian Ten Commandments by a government entity provided the official support of religion "that the Establishment Clause prohibits." Official display of the Nativity Scene here is far more sectarian than the mere posting of the Ten Commandments since the Nativity Scene constitutes a state celebration and symbolic affirmation of the Divine nature of the Christ Child.

The Establishment Clause also "mandates governmental neutrality." It accordingly is constitutionally impermissible to discriminate among religions generally by disfavoring less established religions, and it is similarly discriminatory to give favored status to a majority religion such as Christianity.

Most basically, the City's display of an overtly religious symbol violates the three tests set forth in *Lemon v. Kurtzman*. First, although the City must establish that its display has a secular purpose, the record here compels the conclusion that the very purpose of the Nativity scene is religious. One of the primary reasons for the City's maintenance of the Nativity scene is to "keep Christ in Christmas." Second, the record compels the conclusion that the effect of the City's display of the Nativity scene—on adults and particularly on impressionable children—is instead the advancement of Christian religion. Third, the government's choosing to display the symbols of one religion invokes the "competition among religious sects for political and religious supremacy" which the Establishment Clause guards against. Given the divisiveness evident in Pawtucket, the record here reveals impermissible excessive entanglement.

Unlike the legislative chaplaincy at issue in *Marsh v. Chambers,* no historical exception can be utilized to shield the practice from doctrinal scrutiny. In *Marsh* the brief submitted by the United States pointed out repeated instances of the toleration of paid legislative chaplains by the Founders. However, no similar historical evidence may be marshalled in favor of a practice of publicly-funded sectarian religious displays. The Solicitor General's brief in this case cannot point to a single instance in which the Founders countenanced the use of public funds to erect avowedly sectarian religious symbols at Christmas time or at any other time.

In sum, whether viewed as placing the imprimatur of the state on sectarian belief as in *Stone v. Graham,* as subject to the strict scrutiny test applied in discriminatory contexts such as in *Larson v. Valente,* or under the traditional three-part test of *Lemon v. Kurtzman,* the expenditure of public funds to purchase, maintain and display the Nativity scene does not withstand Establishment Clause analysis.

The arguments of the three Jewish organizations and the Churches of Christ in support of the ACLU developed the issue of the Nativity scene's impact on minority religious sects and Christians who find government use of religious symbols offensive.[17]

It is because of the fundamentally religious nature of the Creche that the sensibilities of non-Christian Americans and Christians who are offended by such use of a religious symbol must be recognized. Nor do we believe we are being hyper-sensitive or overly fastidious in this regard. On the contrary, it was protection against just such dangers, not only to Jews but to Christian and other religious sects as well, that led to the promulgation of the Establishment Clause itself.

Pawtucket's Nativity Scene sends a clear message of isolation to Jewish citizens. This occurs because the Nativity scene is a symbol of the divinity of the birth of Jesus, the Christian Messiah, which throughout the ages has highlighted the historic difference between Jews and Christians—failure by Jews to accept Jesus as the Messiah. Recounting the birth of the Christian Messiah, the Nativity scene evokes the question that has "haunted Jewish–Christian relations for nearly two milennia. . . . "What were the [Jews'] motives for rejecting the messianic claims made about Jesus?" Because the Nativity scene is the symbol of the gulf between Christians and Jews, Pawtucket's sponsorship of the Nativity scene will only serve to further cause divisiveness in the community, which will lead to increasing government entanglement in religion as competing religious groups seek to have a government endorsement of their religious symbols.

Moreover, we would also note that the commercial use made of the Creche by the municipality fosters a different kind of entanglement, to wit, the misappropriation by the State for its secular purposes of sacred symbols thought to be reserved for religious purposes. Thus, the primary use here made of the Creche, to attract shoppers, might well be viewed by many devout Christians as a profanation, detracting from the religious significance of the Nativity scene. Such misuse of religion is as fully prohibited by the Establishment Clause as any activity which intends to endorse religion.

ORAL ARGUMENT

On Tuesday, 4 October 1983, at 10:03 A.M., the second day of the 1983–1984 Supreme Court term, the nine black-robed justices, led by the chief justice, filed into the courtroom and seated themselves in plush high-backed chairs on an elevated dais. Chief Justice Burger was seated in the center; the other justices were flanked beside him in declining order of seniority. The marshal called the Court to order. "Oyez, oyez, oyez! All persons having business before the Honorable, the Supreme Court of the United States, are admonished to draw near and give their attention, for the Court is now sitting. God save the United States and this Honorable Court." Beseeching God's help for country and Court would have special relevance on this particular day.

Oral argument is the only publicly visible part of the Court's decision-making process. It is a time for lawyers on both sides to present their legal positions, but also an occasion for the justices to ask questions and to request additional information. The process has been described as formally informal. In times past it was not uncommon for the oratory to last several hours or even days. Today, however, except in cases of extraordinary public importance, the practice is to limit each side's discussion time to thirty minutes. Time limits are rigidly enforced. A white light flashes five minutes before time is to expire. When the light turns red, the lawyer must stop.

Even for the most experienced attorneys, arguing before the Supreme Court is a time of great anxiety. Interruptions for questions from the justices often deflect litigants from their prepared remarks. "Unfriendly" justices may use the time to alert their colleagues to a troublesome part of an argument. Justices who have not made up their minds may raise questions on the part of the case that is causing them the most difficulty. Occasionally "friendly" justices will steer an attorney to the arguments they think will most help his or her cause. The questions asked are frequently technical and often require attorneys to speculate about hypothetical variations on the case under discussion. To be effective in this highly interactive process, attorneys must be able to think on their feet.

Although the justices come to the oral argument well briefed on the cases, oral argument sometimes makes the difference. Chief Justice Rehnquist recently noted, "In a significant minority of the cases in which I have heard oral argument, I have left the bench feeling different about the case than I did when I came on the bench."[18] For justices who may be less versed in certain areas of the law and for members of the Court who comprise the "swing vote," the one hour of presentation and debate may be decisive. Cases are won or lost in the courtroom. Well-prepared litigants will have mastered not only the legal arguments to support their positions, but also will be familiar with the background and judicial philosophy of each of the justices.

In focusing on the Court's membership, Alan Westin has observed that the student of the constitutional process "looks for the interaction in each case of the justice's personal views on the subject, his fidelity to the Court's case precedents in that area, and his definition of the proper role for the judiciary in this context."[19] Although this information in itself may not be enough to predict conclusively how a justice will vote in all instances, it helps to identify the general "political" context in which the case will be decided.

One student of the Constitution categorizes the qualifications of Supreme Court justices as "representational, professional, and doctrinal."[20] The major representational qualifications presidents look for in Court nominees is political party.

Over 90 percent of the justices have been of the same party affiliation as the presidents who appointed them.

Although the typical Supreme Court justice is often described as white, male, Protestant, and from the East, ethnic, religious, and geographical balance on the Court may also be important. In the past, Court observers have talked about a "Catholic seat," a "Jewish seat," and a "Western seat." Thurgood Marshall's elevation to the Court in 1967, the first black nomination, added a new representational dimension to the process. Similarly, the first woman justice, Sandra Day O'Connor (1981), and the first Italian American, Antonin Scalia (1986), are recent examples of judicial nominations with representational implications.

The professional qualifications of judicial nominees relate to judicial or governmental service. A significant majority of Supreme Court justices have served either on the federal court of appeals or on a state supreme court prior to being nominated to the Supreme Court. Those without prior judicial experience have commonly served in the Justice Department or were distinguished attorneys.

Because the Court's decisions often affect their legislative programs and the general goals of their administrations, presidents also look to ideology in making appointments to the Supreme Court. Although it is not possible to predict with complete accuracy how a justice will behave on the bench, presidents generally have been very successful in identifying the ideological predispositions of their nominees. With his appointments Franklin Roosevelt transformed the High Court from a laissez-faire-oriented group of justices to one that was in complete accord with his liberal economic policies. Recent Republican presidents, most notably Ronald Reagan and Richard Nixon, have successfully used their appointments to shore up the conservative "self-restraint" bloc on the Court.

To appreciate *Lynch v. Donnelly* fully, then, it is important to understand the backgrounds and doctrinal predispositions of the justices who would rule on the fate of the Nativity scene. A brief biographical sketch of the nine justices is followed by an analysis of their voting behavior on establishment cases.

The "Lynch" Court

WARREN E. BURGER, chief justice. Born 1907. Republican, appointed by President Nixon to succeed Earl Warren in 1969. He attended the University of Minnesota and received his law degree from St. Paul College of Law. A political supporter of Dwight Eisenhower in 1952, he was first appointed assistant attorney general (1953–1956) and then nominated by President Eisenhower to the Washington, D.C. Court of Appeals (1956–1969). A conservative, he was appointed to the Court in part for his philosophy of judicial self-restraint. Burger customarily wrote the Court's opinion on major cases in which he was aligned with the majority. He resigned from the Court in 1986 and was succeeded as chief justice by William Rehnquist.

WILLIAM J. BRENNAN, JR., senior associate justice. Born 1906. Democrat, appointed by President Eisenhower in 1956 (one of two current justices appointed by a president of the opposite party). He graduated from the University of Pennsylvania and received a law degree from Harvard University. He served as a justice on the supreme court of New Jersey prior to his elevation to the Supreme Court. At the time of this writing he is one of the most liberal activist justices. When the Nativity scene was considered, Brennan was the only Catholic on the Court. His eight colleagues were all Protestant.

BYRON R. WHITE. Born 1917. Democrat, appointed by President Kennedy in 1962. After graduating from the University of Colorado, he was a Rhodes Scholar and played professional football. His law degree is from Yale University. He worked actively in the 1960 presidential election campaign for Kennedy, after which he was named deputy attorney general (1961–1962). He has surprised Court observers by his conservative views, particularly on First Amendment issues.

THURGOOD MARSHALL. Born 1908. Democrat, appointed by President Johnson in 1967. The only black ever to serve on the Court, Marshall is a graduate of Lincoln University (A.B.) and Howard University (LL.B.) He worked for the NAACP (1936–1961) until he was appointed to the Second Circuit Court of Appeals in 1961. He was appointed solicitor general of the United States in 1965. Marshall is almost always aligned with Brennan in the liberal activist bloc of judges.

HARRY A. BLACKMUN. Born 1908. Republican, appointed by President Nixon in 1970. He earned undergraduate and law degrees at Harvard University. He served on the Eighth Circuit Court of Appeals from 1959–1970. A childhood friend of Justice Burger, Blackmun has moderated his own conservative ideological position during his tenure on the Court. He is generally characterized as "independent" and "moderately liberal on civil rights."

WILLIAM H. REHNQUIST. Born 1925. Republican, appointed by President Nixon in 1971. He received his undergraduate and law school training at Stanford University. He was a "Goldwater" Republican, law and order proponent, and outspoken critic of the Supreme Court of the fifties and sixties. He practiced law in Phoenix, Arizona, until his appointment as assistant attorney general (1969–1971). One of three sitting justices without prior judicial experience, he is generally regarded as the most conservative member of the Court and the strongest opponent of "judicial policy making." President Reagan elevated him to the chief justiceship in 1986. Justice Antonin Scalia replaced Rehnquist as associate justice.

LEWIS F. POWELL, JR.   Born 1907. Southern Democrat, appointed by Nixon in 1972. He graduated from Washington and Lee University and received a law degree from Harvard University. A Richmond, Virginia, lawyer for most of his career, he had served as chairman of the Richmond school board and as president of the American Bar Association before his appointment to the Court. He had no prior judicial experience. A moderate "consensus builder," he came to be recognized as the Court's swing vote on many issues. Powell resigned in 1987 and was replaced by Justice Anthony M. Kennedy.

JOHN P. STEVENS.   Born 1920. Republican, appointed by President Ford in 1975. He has an undergraduate degree from the University of Chicago and a law degree from Northwestern University. A law professor and practicing attorney for most of his career, he was appointed to the Seventh Circuit Court of Appeals in 1970. Stevens' ideological leanings have been hard to characterize. He is generally described as "nondoctrinaire" and "moderate." On civil liberties issues he is generally aligned with the liberals.

SANDRA DAY O'CONNOR.   Born 1930. Republican, appointed by President Reagan in 1981. She is the youngest member of the Court and the only woman ever to be appointed. Like Rehnquist, she received her undergraduate and law school training at Stanford University. She was elected to the Arizona state senate (1967–1975) and served as a superior court judge (1975–1979) and court of appeals judge (1979–1981) in Arizona before her appointment to the Supreme Court. Her advance billing was that of a moderate conservative exponent of judicial self-restraint.

Table 3 reports the voting behavior and opinion-writing activity of the members of the "*Lynch*" Court on establishment-of-religion cases in which they participated. Three voting blocs emerge from the analysis. One group, consisting of justices Brennan, Marshall, and Stevens, has voted most often against government involvement in religious matters; they have formed the "separationist" bloc. Justices White, Burger, Rehnquist, and O'Connor have voted most often with the government in its efforts to accommodate religion; they have constituted the "accommodationist" bloc. Justices Powell and Blackmun have appeared to have less well defined positions; they have been the "swing votes."

TABLE 3. ESTABLISHMENT VOTES BY *LYNCH* COURT JUSTICES

	No. cases	Sep. votes	Accom. votes	% Votes in majority	Written opinions
Separationists					
Brennan	19	16	3	58%	10 (6 dissent.)
Marshall	16	14	2	50%	2 (2 dissent.)
Stevens	8	7	1	50%	4 (4 dissent.)
Swing Votes					
Blackmun	13	7	6	54%	3 (1 dissent.)
Powell	11	7	4	100%	2 (1 dissent.)
Accommodationists					
White	17	5	12	76%	6 (3 dissent.)
Burger	14	2	12	78%	7 (2 dissent.)
Rehnquist	11	0	11	64%	5 (4 dissent.)
O'Connor	3	0	3	67%	0

The Court has been badly divided on establishment cases. Note the number of dissenting opinions that have been written. In the fourteen cases to come down since Justice Burger was seated, seven cases were decided by 5–4 votes; four others were 6–3 majorities. Justices Brennan and Stevens have been the most prolific opinion writers for the separationists. Chief Justice Burger and Justice White have been the leading spokesmen for the "accommodationists." The "swing" voters have tended not to write as many opinions. Very important, however, is the fact that despite a fractured Court, Justice Powell has voted with the majority on every establishment case in which he has participated. His vote was controlling in most of those decisions.

The Petitioners' Case

William F. MacMahon, attorney for Pawtucket, was the first to address the Court. Because he had relinquished ten minutes of petitioner's time to Solictor General Lee, MacMahon's allotted time for oral argument was limited to twenty minutes. During that time he was interrupted for questioning by the justices on eight occasions. Not surprisingly the justices were most troubled by the religious nature of the creche and the issue of its "context" in the display.

Justice O'Connor, the most active of the justices in the debate, pursued the "context" question in some detail. Although she clearly understood Pawtucket's position, she appeared to be troubled by a situation in which a Navitity scene might be displayed alone. When pressed on the issue, MacMahon indicated that the creche had become a symbol of what is a national secular holiday and that it would still be permissible as a symbol of Christmas.

The most relentless questioning from the "separationists" came from Justice Marshall, who was clearly disturbed by the religious nature of the creche. The following excerpt from the transcript illustrates the kind of interchange between justices and attorney that occurs during oral argument. Note also how MacMahon attempts to cast his responses with reference to prior establishment rulings.

JUSTICE MARSHALL: What meaning does the creche have other than religion?

MACMAHON: It is a symbol of Christmas, Justice. It is a symbol of Christmas as other secular symbols are.

MARSHALL: Recognized by all religions?

MACMAHON: No, but Christmas . . .

MARSHALL: I didn't think it was.

MACMAHON: Christmas itself . . .

MARSHALL: It is one religion, isn't it?

MACMAHON: Christmas itself is, Justice, yes.

MARSHALL: Christmas itself?

MACMAHON: The holiday of Christmas is a denominational holiday. Sunday is a denominational day. The recognition of Sunday in McGowan against Maryland was not inhibited by the fact that Sunday is a religious day only for certain denominations, and it is a benefit only to . . .

MARSHALL: You mean other denominations other than Christians don't give presents, drink liquor, and have a ball on Christmas?

MACMAHON: That is because it is secular, Justice, yes.

MARSHALL: Well, now, a minute ago you said it was religious. Now you say it is secular.

MACMAHON: No, Justice, it is a dominantly secular holiday in its contemporary celebration. It has religious roots and some religious components. The religious components are part and parcel of the . . .

MARSHALL: My question is, according to your argument, is it religious or secular?

MACMAHON: The holiday, Justice, or the creche?

MARSHALL: Either.

MACMAHON: The holiday is a dominantly secular holiday with a religious origin and some religious component. The creche is a dual symbol. It is a religious symbol and it is also a holiday symbol. Which meaning predominates depends on the setting . . .

MARSHALL: It is part religious.

MACMAHON: Oh, certainly.

MARSHALL: And the state is giving money to a religion?

MACMAHON: The state is celebrating the traditions of the American people, Justice.

MARSHALL: They are giving money to celebrating a religious event.

MACMAHON: Well, perhaps in the same way that the practice of paid chaplaincies is giving money to subsidize that particular religious activity. We would say it is not the subsidization of religion, but it is the subsidization of a secular national folk festival which contains a religious element.

Solictor General Lee, representing the Reagan administration, argued forcefully on behalf of the constitutionality of Pawtucket's actions. The government's position was that as long as the celebration of Christmas as a national holiday was not an establishment of religion, the noncoercive acknowledgment of one of its most recognized symbols was also constitutional. Lee argued that the First Amendment would be "positively offended" by a decision that said Christmas could be announced in every respect but in its religious elements.

In her questioning of Lee, Justice O'Connor revealed some misgivings about the tripartite *Lemon* test. Acknowledging some frustration in coming up with a better alternative, the solicitor general agreed with O'Connor that it would be preferable to read the purpose-and-effect parts of the test together. Utilizing this interpretation, the government would have to show only that its purpose was secular. Almost by definition a legitimate secular purpose could not yield a primary effect that advances religion. Government's efforts to accommodate religion would be easier to sustain.

The Respondents' Reply

Although the Court must decide a case on the basis of the facts presented before it, justices are also mindful that their decisions are precedent-setting rulings for lower courts. Ideally a Supreme Court decision should clarify rather than confuse the law. The difficulties of *Lynch v. Donnelly* were suggested by the Court's questioning of ACLU attorney DeLuca. As he attempted to review the main points of the ACLU case, the attorney was repeatedly interrupted with questions.

DeLuca was asked to react to a number of hypothetical extensions to the facts in the case. The questions listed below are indicative of some of the troubling aspects of the case for the justices and also the complexity of the constitutional issue with which the Court was grappling. Attorney DeLuca's responses are also appended.

Q. If the city did not own the creche, so that everything, including the creche, were privately owned, it wouldn't violate the First Amendment, the fact that it was right next door to City Hall, would it? (DeLuca: Yes, by its proximity to City Hall it would still give the appearance of governmental sponsorship.)

Q. Several years ago Pope John Paul II said mass on the Mall [Washington, D.C.], which is federal property. Would you say that was a step toward establishment of religion? (DeLuca: If the government expended funds for police, traffic control, cleaning up, etc., it probably was unconstitutional.)

Q. Could the city display religious paintings or artifacts in its museum? (DeLuca: Yes, the primary purpose in this instance is to educate rather than to endorse a particular religion.)

Q. Would the city be allowed to erect a cross or a crucifix at Easter? (DeLuca: No.)

Q. Suppose the creche was just one ornament on the Christmas tree and you could hardly see it unless you looked very closely, would that be illegal? (DeLuca: Yes, it is still an acknowledgment of a religious belief.)

Q. Would the display up on the frieze in the courtroom of the Ten Commandments be unconstitutional? (DeLuca: No, it is intended to suggest the beginning of the codification of law.)

At 11:01 A.M., the red light flashed. Chief Justice Burger said, "Thank you, gentlemen. The case is submitted."

Despite the fact that both parties remained convinced that the weight of the evidence was on their side, the lively interchange during oral argument left a number of questions in the minds of the participants. Was Justice O'Connor's active participation an indication that her position in support of the "accommodationists" was not firm? More important, the session gave no clue as to Justice Powell's thinking, even though attorneys on both sides were aware, on the basis of past decisions, that his vote would be crucial to the result.

Which of the four possible standards of judgment or precedent would the Court adopt in deciding the case? If they followed the "strict scrutiny" test of the court of appeals, the ACLU would almost surely prevail. The record did not support a "compelling" governmental interest in displaying the creche. A decision that relied heavily on the "Ten Commandments" precedent, the only case involving the display of a religious symbol to be decided by the Court, would also probably affirm the results of the lower courts. A case could be made that the display of the creche was as much intended to convey a religious message as the posting of the Commandments.

If the Court followed the reasoning of the solictor general that the "long standing historical acceptance" precedent of *Marsh* provided sufficient justification to support Pawtucket's forty-year tradition, the city would be likely to win its appeal. The celebration of Christmas in the United States could be viewed to be as traditional as publicly supported legislative and military chaplains. The outcome of a decision that relied on the traditional Lemon Test would be the most difficult to predict. Both sides appeared to make convincing arguments that on all three parts of the test the result was supportive of their position. A decision based upon *Lemon* might very well turn on whether the justices viewed the creche in isolation or in the context of Pawtucket's total Christmas display.

JUDICIAL CONFERENCE

The judicial conference remains something of a mystery to students of the Supreme Court. When the buzzer sounds summoning the justices to the conference room next to the chief justice's chambers, a highly confidential part of the decision-making process is about to begin. The nine justices are the only individuals permitted to attend the conference. To prevent untimely "leaks" about forthcoming decisions and to demonstrate that the justices "do their own work," law clerks, secretaries, and other court personnel are excluded. The most junior justice serves as messenger and is responsible for communicating the Court's actions to the clerks' offices. What we know of the events that take place behind those closed doors comes largely from the reports of the justices themselves.

During the two-week cycle when the Court hears oral arguments, conferences are held on Wednesday afternoons to discuss and decide Monday's cases, and all day Friday to consider Tuesday's and Wednesday's cases. *Lynch v. Donnelly* was discussed and voted upon on Friday, 7 October 1983.

When the justices are all assembled, tradition dictates that they all shake hands with each other. The custom is repeated at the end of each conference session. The members are seated around a twelve-foot-long mahogany conference table. On the October 1983 day when the Nativity scene case was discussed, Chief Justice Burger sat at one end of the table and Brennan, the senior associate justice, sat at the other end. The three associate justices next in seniority, White, Marshall, and Blackmun, were aligned on one side of the table. The four junior justices, Powell, Rehnquist, Stevens, and O'Connor, were on the opposite side.

The chief justice controls the conference agenda. He begins the discussion of each case by reviewing the facts and lower court actions, after which he outlines his own understanding of the applicable case law. He then indicates whether he will vote to affirm or reverse the lower court decision. Although the voting power of the chief justice is no greater than that of an associate justice, the opportunity to speak and vote first may enhance his ability to influence his colleagues.

Court scholars have noted that the power wielded by a chief justice is as much a function of his personality and leadership style as it is of his position. David Danelski used Chief Justice Charles Evans Hughes to illustrate the potential leadership power in the position. Hughes was an effective "task" leader who used his "intellectual persuasion" and mastery of cases to influence other justices to vote with him. In addition, he dominated the Court in his role as "social" leader by using tactics of friendship, courtesy, and kindness to build support for himself and his judicial philosophy.[21] The extent to which other chiefs have been able to parlay their intellectual and social skills into power on the Court is a matter of conjecture. Chief Justice Burger, it is safe to say, did not compare favorably with Hughes as a dominating force on the Court.

Following Justice Burger, the discussion proceeded to Justice Brennan and down the line to Justice O'Connor. Each justice is generally permitted to speak without interruption. Chief Justice Rehnquist recently noted his "surprise and disappointment at how little interplay there is between the various justices during the process of conferring on a case."[22] This observation contradicts the conventional view that conferences are marked by informality and vigorous give-and-take. Rehnquist laments the fact that, while junior justices have the opportunity to comment upon the views of their senior colleagues, the arguments of the newer members seldom are discussed. The current chief justice would prefer a more "free-wheeling" exchange of views.

After all members have spoken, the chief justice brings the discussion to an end. In most cases a clear position to affirm or reverse the lower court's ruling will have emerged. A formal vote is taken only if the issue remains in doubt. The initial vote in conference does not permanently bind a justice. It is possible that during the opinion-writing stage one or more of the justices may be persuaded to change their minds. The conference vote is important, however, because it will determine who will be assigned the task of writing the Court's opinion.

Chief Justice Rehnquist states that "the signed opinions produced by each Justice are to a very large extent the only visible record of his work on the Court, and the office offers no greater reward than the opportunity to author an opinion on an important point of constitutional law."[23] When the chief justice votes with the majority, he makes the opinion assignment. He may decide to write it himself, or give it to another member of the majority. When the chief justice is in the minority, the senior associate justice in the majority makes the assignment.

A number of factors can influence the opinion assignment process. An attempt is made to balance the opinion-writing workload among the nine members. Some justices, recognized for a particular specialization, may be asked to write in that area. In cases that are closely decided, a moderate judge whose opinion can forge an acceptable consensus may be recruited to write. The chief justice traditionally writes for the Court in important "landmark" decisions.

The justice selected to write the majority opinion speaks not only for himself, but also for the other justices aligned on his side. Because the oral presentations of the members at conference do not always clearly settle exactly how the opinion will be reasoned through, the opinion writer must be careful not to lose the support of his colleagues by drafting an opinion that does not accurately express their views. On some occasions it happens that judges voting with either the majority or the minority in conference will change their minds after reading a proposed opinion. In close cases these vote switches can even change the result that was reached in conference.

With the assistance of law clerks, the justice prepares a draft opinion, which is sent to all members for their comments. In many cases the majority will accept the first version. However, when one or more justices object to a proposed opinion, a process of bargaining and negotiation takes place among the justices in an effort to reach an acceptable compromise. The long-term significance of a case will depend in part on the degree of unanimity the Court can achieve.

Chief Justice Rehnquist comments on the opinion-writing process:

> Circulate [opinion drafts] to other chambers we do, and we wait anxiously to see what the reaction of the other Justices will be, especially those Justices who voted with the majority at conference. If a Justice agrees with the draft and has no criticism or suggestions, he will send a letter saying something such as "Please join me in your opinion in this case." If a Justice agrees with the general import of the draft, but wishes changes to be made in it before joining, a letter to that effect will be sent, and the writer will, if

possible, accommodate the suggestions. The willingness to accommodate on the part of the author of an opinion is often directly proportional to the number of votes supporting the majority result at conference; if there are only five justices voting to affirm the decision of the lower court, and one of those five wishes significant changes to be made in the draft, the opinion writer is under considerable pressure to work out something that will satisfy the critic, in order to obtain five votes for the opinion. . . . But if the result at conference was reached by a unanimous or lopsided vote, a critic who wishes substantial changes in the opinion has less leverage.[24]

The majority opinion may be accompanied by two other kinds of opinions. A justice who agrees with the majority on the result of the case but who differs with all or part of the reasoning expressed in the Court's opinion may write a "concurring opinion." Although they do not change the result of the case, concurring opinions may weaken precedential value of a ruling by demonstrating that the Court's explanation for a ruling is fragmented. Justices who disagree with the majority may write a "dissenting opinion," expressing the reasons why they oppose the Court's ruling. Dissenting opinions are an important part of the judicial process because the reasoning of dissenting justices may be persuasive to succeeding Courts. When Supreme Court precedents are overruled, the Court will often use a dissenting opinion as a point of departure.

Written opinions are the Court's principal method to express itself to the nation. The most important function of the Court's statement is to guide other judges in their efforts to decide similar cases. Some opinions are directed at elected officials, suggesting an appropriate action that they might wish to take to correct an unconstitutional practice. Equally important, the Court's opinions are a method to communicate with and educate the public. One Court scholar has observed that "the Supreme Court is an educational body, and the justices are inevitably teachers in a vital national seminar."[25]

The time involved in the opinion-writing stage in a case can be lengthy, particularly if the Court is badly divided. Although the impact of a case is related to the kind of consensus the Court can muster, it is rare for the Court to decide a case 9–0. A 5–4 vote with multiple opinions, on the other hand, does little to settle the law. All of the establishment-of-religion cases prior to *Lynch v. Donnelly* included at least one dissenting voice.

At the Friday conferences, the first order of business for the justices is to decide which opinions are ready to be announced. If the writer of the majority opinion reports that all of the votes are in, unless there is some objection, the Court will make public its decision from the bench the following week. The opinion's author will describe the case, summarize the reasoning of the majority, announce the result, and report any concurring or dissenting opinions. Copies of the full text of the opinion are available from the clerk's office on the day the decision is reported.

Because it had adjusted its calendar to make room for the oral argument in the Nativity scene case in early October during the first week of the new term, the Court appeared to want to settle the question in time for Christmas 1983. The *New York Times* reported rumors in mid-December that the decision was about to come down. Christmas came and went, however, without a ruling.

On 5 March 1984, three years, two months, and seventeen days after the ACLU had filed suit in federal district court, the Supreme Court handed down its ruling. By a 5–4 vote, the Court reversed the decisions of the lower courts, ruling the Nativity scene in Pawtucket's Christmas display did not violate the First Amendment. Chief Justice Burger wrote the majority opinion for himself and Justices White, Powell, Rehnquist, and O'Connor. Justice O'Connor wrote a separate concurring opinion. Justice Brennan, joined by Justices Marshall, Blackmun, and Stevens, dissented. Justice Blackmun also penned a brief dissent.

Excerpts from the majority opinion and from Justice Brennan's dissent are included below. Summaries of Justice O'Connor's concurring opinion and Blackmun's dissent are also appended.[26]

THE DECISION

Chief Justice Burger, expressing the views of Justices White, Powell, Rehnquist, and O'Connor, delivered the opinion of the Court:

A.

In every Establishment Clause case, we must reconcile the inescapable tension between the objective of preventing unnecessary intrusion of either the church or the state upon each other, and the reality that, as the Court has so often noted, total separation of the two is not possible. The Court has sometimes described the Religion Clauses as erecting a "wall" between church and state. The concept of a "wall" is a useful figure of speech probably deriving from views of Thomas Jefferson. The metaphor has served as a reminder that the Establishment Clause forbids an established church or anything approaching it. But the metaphor itself is not a wholly accurate description of the practical aspects of the relationship that in fact exists between church and state.

No significant segment of our society and no institution within it can exist in a vacuum or in total or absolute isolation from all the other parts, much less from government. Nor does the Constitution require complete separation of church and state; it affirmatively mandates accommodation, not merely tolerance, of all religions, and forbids hostility toward any. Indeed, we have observed, such hostility would bring us into "war with our national tradition as embodied in the First Amendment's guarantee of the free exercise of religion."

B.

The Court's interpretation of the Establishment Clause has comported with what history reveals was the contemporaneous understanding of its guarantees. A significant example of the contemporaneous understanding of the Clause is found in the events of the first week of the First Session of the First Congress in 1789. In the very week that Congress approved the Establishment Clause as part of the Bill of Rights for submission to the states, it enacted legislation providing for paid chaplains for the House and Senate. In *Marsh v. Chambers* we noted that seventeen Members of the First Congress had been Delegates to the Constitutional Convention where freedom of speech, press, and religion and antagonism toward an established church were subjects of frequent discussion. We saw no conflict with the Establishment Clause when Nebraska employed members of the clergy as official Legislative Chaplains to give opening prayers at sessions of the state legislature.

It is clear that neither the seventeen draftsmen of the Constitution who were members of the First Congress, nor the Congress of 1789, saw any establishment problem in the employment of congressional chaplains to offer daily prayers in the Congress, a practice that has continued for nearly two centuries. It would be difficult to identify a more striking example of the accommodation of religious belief intended by the Framers.

C.

There is an unbroken history of official acknowledgement by all three branches of government of the role of religion in American life from at least 1789. Our history is replete with official references to the value and invocation of Divine guidance in deliberations and pronouncements of the Founding Fathers and contemporary leaders. President Washington and his successors proclaimed Thanksgiving, with all its religious overtones, a day of national celebration and Congress made it a national holiday more than a century ago. That holiday has not lost its theme of expressing thanks for Divine aid any more than has Christmas lost its religious significance.

By Acts of Congress, it has long been the practice that federal employees are released from duties on the national holidays, while being paid from the same public revenues that provided the compensation of the Chaplains of the Senate and the House and the military services. Thus it is clear that Government has long recognized—indeed it has subsidized—holidays with religious significance.

Other examples of reference to our religious heritage are found in the statutorily prescribed national motto "In God We Trust," and in the language "One Nation Under God," as a part of the Pledge of Allegiance to the American Flag. The National Gallery in Washington, maintained with Government support, has long exhibited masterpieces with explicit Christian themes and messages. The very chamber in which oral arguments on this case were heard is decorated with a notable and permanent—not seasonal—symbol of religion: Moses with Ten Commandments. Congress has long provided chapels in the Capitol for religious worship and meditation. Congress has directed the President to proclaim a National Day of Prayer each year "on which [day] the people of the United States may turn to God in prayer and meditation at churches, in groups, and as individuals."

One cannot look at even this brief resume without finding that our history is pervaded by expressions of religious beliefs. Governmental action has "followed the best of our traditions" and "respected the religious nature of our people."

D.

This history may help explain why the Court consistently has declined to take a rigid, absolutist view of the Establishment Clause. Rather than mechanically invalidating all governmental conduct or statutes that confer benefits or give special recognition to religion in general or to one faith—as an absolutist approach would dictate—the Court has scrutinized challenged legislation or official conduct to determine whether, in reality, it establishes a religion or religious faith, or tends to do so.

In each case, the inquiry calls for line drawing; no fixed, per se rule can be framed. The line between permissible relationships and those barred by the Clause can no more be straight and unwavering than due process can be defined in a single stroke or phrase or test. The clause erects a "blurred, indistinct, and variable barrier depending on all the circumstances of a particular relationship."

In the line-drawing process we have often found it useful to inquire whether the challenged law or conduct has a secular purpose, whether its principal or primary effect is to advance or inhibit religion, and whether it creates an excessive entanglement of government with religion. In this case, the focus of our inquiry must be on the creche in the context of the Christmas season. In *Stone,* for example, we invalidated a state statute requiring the posting of a copy of the Ten Commandments on public classroom walls. But the Court carefully pointed out that the Commandments were posted purely as a religious admonition, not "integrated into the school curriculum, where the Bible may be used in an appropriate study of history, civilization, ethics, comparative religion, or the like." The Court has invalidated legislation or governmental action on the ground that a secular purpose was lacking, but only when it has concluded there was no question that the statute of activity was motivated wholly by religious considerations.

The District Court inferred from the religious nature of the creche that the City has no secular purpose for the display. In so doing, it rejected the City's claim that its reasons for including the creche are essentially the same reasons for sponsoring the display as a whole. The District Court plainly erred by focusing almost exclusively on the creche. When viewed in the proper context of the Christmas Holiday season, it is apparent that, on this record, there is insufficient evidence to establish that the inclusion of the creche is a purposeful or surreptitious effort to express some kind of subtle governmental advocacy of a particular religious message. In a pluralistic society a variety of motives and purposes are implicated. The City, like the Congresses and Presidents, however, has principally taken note of a significant historical religious event long celebrated in the Western World.

The display is sponsored by the City to celebrate the Holiday and to depict the origins of that Holiday. These are legitimate secular purposes.

The District Court found that the primary effect of including the creche is to confer a substantial benefit on religion in general and on the Christian faith in particular. Comparisons of the relative benefits to religion of different forms of government support are elusive and difficult to make. We are unable to discern a greater aid to religion deriving from inclusion of the creche than from the benefits and endorsements previously held not violative of the Establishment Clause. The City's inclusion of the creche "merely happens to coincide or harmonize with the tenets of some religions."

The dissent asserts some observers may perceive that the City has aligned itself with the Christian faith by including a Christian symbol in its display and that this serves to advance religion. We can assume, *arguendo*, that the display advances religion in a sense; but our precedents plainly contemplate that on occasion some advancement of religion will result from governmental action. Here, whatever benefit to one faith or religion or to all religions, is indirect, remote and incidental; display of the creche is no more an advancement or endorsement of religion than the Congressional and Executive recognition of the origins of the Holiday itself as "Christ's Mass," or the exhibition of literally hundreds of religious paintings in governmentally supported museums.

The District Court went on to hold that some political divisiveness was engendered by this litigation. Coupled with its finding of an impermissible sectarian purpose and effect, this persuaded the court that there was "excessive entanglement." Entanglement is a question of kind and degree. The Court of Appeals correctly observed that this Court has not held that political divisiveness alone can serve to invalidate otherwise permissible conduct. Apart from this litigation there is no evidence of political friction or divisiveness over the creche in the 40-year history of Pawtucket's Christmas celebration. A litigant cannot, by the very act of commencing a lawsuit, create the appearance of divisiveness and then exploit it as evidence of entanglement.

We are satisfied that the City has a secular purpose for including the creche, that the City has not impermissibly advanced religion, and that including the creche does not create excessive entanglement between religion and government.

E.

Justice Brennan describes the creche as a "re-creation of an event that lies at the heart of Christian faith." Of course the creche is identified with one religious faith but no more so than examples we have set out from prior cases in which we found no conflict with the Establishment Clause. To forbid the use of this one passive symbol at the very time people are taking note of the season with Christmas hymns and carols in public schools and other public places, and while the Congress and Legislatures open sessions with prayers by paid chaplains would be a stilted over-reaction contrary to our history and to our holdings. If the presence of the creche in this display violates the Establishment Clause, a host of other forms of taking official note of Christmas, and of our religious heritage, are equally offensive to the Constitution. Any notion that these symbols pose a real danger of establishment of a state church is far-fetched indeed.

Accordingly, the judgement of the Court of Appeals is reversed.

Justice O'Connor wrote a *concurring* opinion suggesting the need for a "clarification of our Establishment Clause doctrine." Submitting that the Lemon standard has never made it clear how the three parts of the test "relate to the principles enshrined in the Establishment Clause," O'Connor focused on the questions of institutional entanglement and on endorsement or disapproval of religion to clarify the test as an analytical device.

In so doing, she reached the same result as the Court. In limiting the entanglement prongs of the test to institutional entanglement, she rejected the notion that political divisiveness can be used as an "independent ground for holding a governmental practice unconstitutional."

The central issue for Justice O'Connor was whether Pawtucket endorsed Christianity by its display of the creche. After careful scrutiny of the practice she found that it was neither "government's actual purpose to endorse religion, nor did its actual effect convey a message of endorsement."

Justice Brennan, joined by Justices Marshall, Blackmun, and Stevens, dissented.

> The Court reaches an essentially narrow result which turns largely upon the particular holiday context in which the City of Pawtucket's Nativity scene appears. The Court's decision leaves open questions concerning the constitutionality of the public display of a creche standing alone, or the public display of other distinctively religious symbols such as a cross. Despite the narrow contours of the Court's opinion, our precedents in my view compel the holding that Pawtucket's inclusion of a life-sized display depicting the biblical description of the birth of Christ as part of its annual Christmas celebration is unconstitutional. Nothing in the history of such practices or the setting in which the city's creche is presented obscures or diminishes the plain fact that Pawtucket's action amounts to an impermissible government endorsement of a particular faith.

> The Court's less than vigorous application of the *Lemon* test suggests that its commitment to those standards may only be superficial. After reviewing the Court's opinion, I am convinced that this case appears hard not because the principles of the decision are obscure, but because the Christmas holiday seems so familiar and agreeable. Although the Court's reluctance to disturb a community's

chosen method of celebrating such an agreeable holiday is understandable, that cannot justify the Court's departure from controlling precedent. In my view, Pawtucket's maintenance and display at public expense of a symbol as distinctively sectarian as a creche simply cannot be squared with our prior cases. And it is plainly contrary to the purposes and values of the Establishment Clause to pretend, as the Court does, that the otherwise secular setting of Pawtucket's Nativity scene dilutes in some fashion that creche's singular religiosity, or that the City's annual display reflects nothing more than an "acknowledgment" of our shared national heritage. Neither the character of the Christmas holiday itself, nor our heritage of religious expression supports this result. Indeed, our remarkable and precious religious diversity as a nation, which the Establishment Clause seeks to protect, runs directly counter to today's decision.

A.

Applying the three-part test to Pawtucket's creche, I am persuaded that the City's inclusion of the creche in its Christmas display does not reflect a "clearly secular purpose." All of Pawtucket's "valid secular objectives can readily be accomplished by other means." Plainly, the City's interest in celebrating the holiday and in promoting both retail sales and goodwill are fully served by the elaborate display of Santa Claus, reindeer, and a wishing well that are already a part of Pawtucket's annual Christmas display. More importantly, the Nativity scene, unlike every other element of the Hodgson Park display, reflects a sectarian exclusivity that the avowed purposes of celebrating the holiday season and promoting retail commerce simply do not encompass. To be found constitutional, Pawtucket's seasonal celebration must at least be non-denominational and not serve to promote religion. The inclusion of a distinctively religious element like the creche, however, demonstrates that a narrower sectarian purpose lay behind the decision to include a Nativity scene. That the creche retained this religious character for the people and municipal government is suggested by the Mayor's testimony at trial in which he stated that for him, as well as others in the City, the effort to eliminate the Nativity scene from Pawtucket's Christmas celebration "is a step towards establishing another religion, non-religion that it may be." Plainly, the City and its leaders understood that the inclusion of the creche in its display would serve the wholly religious purpose of "keeping Christ in Christmas."

The "primary effect" of including a Nativity scene in the City's display is, as the District Court found, to place the government's imprimatur of approval on the particular religious beliefs exemplified by the creche. Those who believe in the message of the Nativity receive the unique and exclusive benefit of public recognition and approval of their views. For many, the City's decision to include the creche as part of its extensive and costly efforts to celebrate Christmas can only mean that the prestige of the government has been conferred on the beliefs associated with the creche, thereby providing a "significant symbolic benefit to religion." The effect on minority religious groups, as well as on those who may reject all religion, is to convey the message that their views are not similarly worthy of public recognition nor entitled to public support. It was precisely this sort of religious chauvinism that the Establishment Clause was intended forever to prohibit.

Finally it is evidence that Pawtucket's inclusion of a creche as part of its annual Christmas display does pose a significant threat of fostering "excessive entanglement." Although no political divisiveness was apparent in Pawtucket prior to the filing of respondents' lawsuit, that act, as the District Court found, unleashed powerful emotional reactions which divided the City along religious lines. The fact that calm had prevailed prior to this suit does not immediately suggest the absence of any division on the point for, as the District Court observed, the quiescence of those opposed to the creche may have reflected nothing more than their sense of futility in opposing the majority. We have repeatedly emphasized that "too close a proximity" between religious and civil authorities may represent a "warning signal" that the values embodied in the Establishment Clause are at risk. Furthermore, the Court should not blind itself to the fact that because communities differ in religious composition, the controversy over whether local governments may adopt religious symbols will continue to fester.

In sum, considering the District Court's careful findings of fact under the three-part analysis called for by our prior cases, I have no difficulty concluding that Pawtucket's display of the creche is unconstitutional.

B.

The Court advances two principal arguments to support its conclusion that the Pawtucket creche satisfies the *Lemon* test. Neither is persuasive.

First. The Court, focusing on the holiday "context" in which the Nativity scene appeared, seeks to explain away the clear religious import of the creche. But it blinks reality to claim that by including such a distinctively religious object as the creche in its Christmas display, Pawtucket has done no more than make use of a "traditional" symbol of the holiday, and has thereby purged the creche of its religious content and conferred only an "incidental and indirect" benefit on religion.

In the first place, the City has positioned the creche in a

central and highly visible location within the Hodgson Park display. Moreover, it has done nothing to disclaim government approval of the religious significance of the creche. Third, we have consistently acknowledged that an otherwise secular setting alone does not suffice to justify a governmental practice that has the effect of aiding religion. Finally, and most importantly, even in the context of Pawtucket's seasonal celebration, the creche retains a specifically Christian religious meaning. I refuse to accept the notion implicit in today's decision that non-Christians would find the religious content of the creche is eliminated by the fact that it appears as part of the City's otherwise secular celebration of the Christmas holiday.

Second. The Court apparently believes that once it finds that the designation of Christmas as a public holiday is constitutionally acceptable, it is then free to conclude that virtually every form of governmental association with the celebration of the holiday is also constitutional. The Court's logic is fundamentally flawed because it blurs the distinction between the secular aspects of Christmas and its distinctively religious character, as exemplified by the creche. To suggest, as the Court does, that such a symbol is merely "traditional" and therefore no different from Santa's house or reindeer is not only offensive to those for whom the creche has profound significance, but insulting to those who insist for religious or personal reasons that the story of Christ is in no sense a part of "history" nor an unavoidable element of our national "heritage."

The fact that Pawtucket has gone to the trouble of making such an elaborate public celebration and of including a creche in an otherwise secular setting inevitably serves to reinforce the sense that the City means to express solidarity with the Christian message of the creche and to dismiss other faiths as unworthy of similar attention and support.

C.

It appears from our prior decisions that at least three principles—tracing the narrow channels which government acknowledgments must follow to satisfy the Establishment Clause—may be identified. First, although the government may not be compelled to do so by the Free Exercise Clause, it may, consistently with the Establishment Clause, act to accommodate to some extent the opportunities of individuals to practice their religion. Second, our cases recognize that while a particular governmental practice may have derived from religious motivations and retain certain religious connotations, it is nonetheless permissible for the government to pursue the practice when it is continued solely for secular purposes. Finally, we have noted that government cannot be completely prohibited from recognizing in its public actions the religious beliefs and practices of the American people as an aspect of our national history and culture.

The creche fits none of these categories. Inclusion of the creche is not necessary to accommodate individual religious expression. Nor is the inclusion of the creche necessary to serve wholly secular goals; it is clear that the City's secular purposes of celebrating the Christmas holiday and promoting retail commerce can be fully served without the creche. And the creche, because of its unique association with Christianity, is clearly more sectarian than those references to God that we accept in ceremonial phrases or in other contexts that assure neutrality.

D.

The American historical experience concerning the public celebration of Christmas, if carefully examined, provides no support for the Court's decision. The opening sections of the Court's opinion, while seeking to rely on historical evidence, do not more than recognize the obvious: because of the strong religious currents that run through our history, an inflexible or absolutist enforcement of the Establishment Clause would be both imprudent and impossible. This observation is at once uncontroversial and unilluminating.

The Court wholly fails to discuss this history of the public celebration of Christmas or the use of publicly-displayed Nativity scenes. The Court, instead, simply asserts, without any historical analysis or support whatsoever, that the now familiar celebration of Christmas springs from an unbroken history of acknowledgement "by the people, by the Executive Branch, by the Congress, and the courts for two centuries." The Court's complete failure to offer any explanation of its assertion is perhaps understandable. First, at the time of the adoption of the Constitution and the Bill of Rights, there was no settled pattern of celebrating Christmas, either as a purely religious holiday or as a public event. Second, the historical evidence, such as it is, offers no uniform pattern of widespread acceptance of the holiday and indeed suggests that the development of Christmas as a public holiday is a comparatively recent phenomenon. The evidence with respect to public financing and support for government display of Nativity scenes is difficult to gauge. It is simply impossible to tell whether the practice ever gained widespread acceptance, much less official endorsement, until the twentieth century.

Our prior decisions which relied upon concrete specific historical evidence to support a particular practice simply have no bearing on the question presented in this case. Contrary to today's careless decision, those prior cases have all recognized that the "illumination" provided by history must always be focused on the particular practice at issue in a given case. Without that guiding principle and the intellectual discipline it imposes, the Court is at sea, free to select random elements of America's history solely to suit the views of five Members of this Court.

E.

Under our constitutional scheme, the role of safeguarding our "religious heritage" and of promoting religious beliefs is reserved as the exclusive prerogative of our nation's churches, religious institutions, and spiritual leaders. Because the Framers of the Establishment Clause understood that "religion is too personal, too sacred, too holy to permit its 'unhallowed perversion' by civil authorities," the clause demands that government play no role in this effort. The City's action should be recognized for what it is: a coercive, though perhaps small, step toward establishing the sectarian preferences of the majority at the expense of the minority, accomplished by placing public facilities and funds in support of the religious symbolism and theological tidings that the creche conveys. That the Constitution sets this realm of thought and feeling apart from the pressures and antagonisms of government is one of its supreme achievements. Regrettably, the Court today tarnishes that achievement.

I dissent.

In a brief dissent Justice Blackmun, joined by Justice Stevens, supported Justice Brennan's dissent by stating that the Court had ignored and distorted the guidelines of the Lemon Test. By putting the Nativity scene in a setting "where Christians feel constrained in acknowledging its symbolic meaning and non-Christians feel alienated by its presence," Pawtucket was "misus[ing] a sacred symbol."

V

THE REACTION

The Establishment Clause of the First Amendment has come
to resemble something that has spent a month in a Cuisinart.
George F. Will

WHEN THE SUPREME COURT HANDS down a decision, an important stage in the process by which the political system
passes judgment on issues of constitutional law is concluded.
For the parties in the Nativity scene dispute the Court ruling created a clear winner and loser. Pawtucket, by prevailing in the
case, regained the right to erect its traditional Christmas display
which included the creche. The ACLU failed in its effort to persuade the Court that the city's sponsorship of the manger scene
was in violation of the Establishment Clause.

A Supreme Court victory, however, should not be the cause
for too much celebration. Despite the fact that *Lynch v. Donnelly*
was surely binding on the parties, the controversy over government's power to acknowledge religious symbols was not muted,
and the issue did not disappear from either the Court's docket or
the larger political agenda.

Very few issues that claim the government's attention are
ever fully resolved. Each stage in the political system's consideration of an issue yields an interim solution to a problem that

will sooner or later be reopened. The development of public policy in the American political system is an incremental process in which all institutions share.

Although an objective of the Supreme Court is to "settle" the law on the issues that come before it, Chief Justice Burger's majority opinion in *Lynch* was not the final answer to government-sponsored Nativity scenes or to "official" recognition of religious symbols. The reaction of the various publics to the ruling and postdecision activities within and outside the courts illustrates that the Supreme Court does not always have the last word on constitutional questions, nor does it function in political isolation. It often happens that Court decisions have the effect of raising questions rather than answering them.

Three conditions appear to influence the degree to which a Court ruling will settle the law. For a decision to have maximum impact it must first be stated so unambiguously that no one could doubt what the Court meant. It must be clear enough to prevent other litigants from arguing that the factual settings in their cases are so different that the decision does not apply to them. Unambiguous Court decisions, however, are the exception rather than the rule. In an effort to reach a consensus, judges are often compelled to take a narrow view which restricts the scope of their rulings. And the Court is also not inclined to broaden its decision by anticipating similar or related legal questions before they are raised in a "real" case. Lacking specific guidance, lower courts sometimes must grapple with judicial standards that are often unclear and illusive.

Second, the Court must be united in its opinion if the decision is to carry the maximum weight. Dissenting opinions, or concurring opinions that indicate serious disagreements on the bench over the results of a case or the standards for reaching a decision, will keep the issue alive. When the addition of a new judge or a situation in which a change of heart on the part of one or two justices might alter the position of the Court, critics of a decision will either bide their time or try to unearth the particular circumstances that might precipitate a Court reversal.

Finally, the public's awareness and acceptance of the Court's decision will influence its impact. Since the Court has no real power to enforce its decisions, it must be successful in persuading those individuals, agencies, and institutions that do have enforcement power to carry out its rulings. An opinion that is widely publicized by the media and criticized by the press, legal community, or the general public has a much greater chance of being resisted than a decision that fails to capture the attention of students of the Court.

As these conditions apply to *Lynch v. Donnelly,* the case does not provide the definitive answer to the constitutionality of Nativity scenes or government sponsorship of religious symbols. The majority opinion was not unambiguous. At the outset of his dissenting opinion, Justice Brennan noted that "the Court's decision leaves open questions concerning the constitutionality of the public display of a creche standing alone, or the public display of other distinctively religious symbols such as a cross."[1] Lower court cases relating to religious symbols increased as a result of *Lynch,* and less than six months after it had approved Pawtucket's display, the Court agreed to hear another Nativity scene case.

The *Lynch* decision also raised doubts about the Court's commitment to the tripartite Lemon Test. The test had not been used in the preceding establishment case, *Marsh v. Chambers,* which had supported Nebraska's right to employ a legislative chaplain. During oral argument and in her concurring opinion in the Nativity scene case, Justice O'Connor specifically expressed doubts about the standard. Did this less-than-enthusiastic application of the most commonly accepted church–state test signal the beginning of a more concerted effort by the Court to overhaul its guidelines? What message was the Court sending to federal judges, government officials, and other individuals with a vested interest in establishment questions?

Unanimity was also lacking. *Lynch v. Donnelly* was another 5–4 decision. And like in so many other Establishment Clause decisions, the vote of Justice Powell was the decisive vote on a badly divided court. The fact that Powell rarely explained his view of establishment of religion in written opinions limited the decision's impact and general applicability in the lower courts. The parties with the power to carry out the wishes of the Supreme Court are left to decide for themselves how the particular nuances of a case will tip the delicate balance that has characterized Court opinions in establishment cases.

Although it had attracted considerable attention before the decision was announced, the Court's opinion in *Lynch* received widespread national media exposure. It received front page coverage in both the *New York Times* and the *Washington Post*. It attracted the attention of many of the nation's major columnists and was subjected to a thorough critique by legal scholars. Religious leaders of all denominations expressed their views of the decision's implications for church–state relationships.

A few individuals praised the decision. However, the overwhelming majority of opinion was critical of the ruling. Pawtucket may have won the right to display the creche, but the Court appeared to have done little to either temper emotions or to clarify what the Constitution means by the establishment of religion. Justice Blackmun was probably correct when he noted in his dissent that "the City has its victory—but it is a Pyrrhic one indeed."[2]

Three aspects of the impact of the Nativity scene decision are discussed below. First, we consider the reactions and retrospective views of the major participants in the case and look at the case's impact in Rhode Island. A second section assesses the national response to the decision. The views of the national press, religious community, and legal establishment are presented. In an effort to measure the impact of the *Lynch* decision on judicial perceptions of the constitutionality of government sponsorship of religious symbols, a final section discusses federal court cases of this nature that followed the Pawtucket decision.

THE RHODE ISLAND REACTION

In the short run, Rhode Island had the most at stake in *Lynch v. Donnelly*. Both sides in the dispute had spent so much time, money, and emotional energy to persuade the courts of their positions, that it is not surprising that public opinion about the decision was as divided as it had been before. The Pawtucket officials who had relentlessly persisted in appealing the case to the Supreme Court were elated and felt a sense of satisfaction that their position had prevailed. Mayor Kinch, whose first action was to announce that the city would again erect a Nativity scene in Hodgson Park in 1984, proclaimed the Court decision as "a triumph for all religious freedom." One of the state's newspapers editorialized that "it was appropriate for the Supreme Court to push aside all objection and confirm that the Pawtucket Nativity Scene . . . was a legitimate expression, one depicting the holiday as history, as a sort of festival symbol."[3] Most citizens probably shared the view of one of the city's attorneys that Pawtucket had "struck a blow for liberty."[4]

The Court's decision did little to silence the Nativity scene's opponents. The ACLU expressed its disappointment with the ruling, noting that the Court seemed to be in such disarray that even the five-judge majority could not agree on the appropriate standards to decide the issue. Most of the state's newspapers and religious leaders echoed the ACLU's dismay with the decision. The sentiment expressed in a *Barrington Times* editorial was typical of press reaction.

Is the Supreme Court decision a victory? Not really. The only people with reason to rejoice are the forces of religious intolerance, those who subscribe to the philosophy of "Christians are the majority and majority rules." No, the decision is really a defeat, not only for religious freedom, but for the Christian religion. For what the decision did is brand the creche a "secular folk art" object. Rather than putting Christ back in Christmas, it took more out, and Christ in Christmas is something that's in short supply these days.[5]

A *Providence Journal* writer concluded, "Pawtucket has won and is free to confront the public with a deflated, downgraded symbol that five justices agree is 'passive' and of no special benefit to religion. Some Christians will ask to be spared any more victories like this."[6]

Although Roman Catholic bishop Louis E. Gelineau was "pleased" by the Court ruling and joined in the "joy" of those who had worked "so diligently to pursue the progress in the case," the majority of Protestant and Jewish leaders in the state objected to the decision. They alleged its effect was to "negate the true meaning of the manger," "permit government to recognize a particular religion," "encourage communities to use religious symbols to promote commercial interests," permit government to "ride roughshod over all minorities," and "trivialize religion."

The reactions and assessment of the three Rhode Island citizens with the greatest personal involvement in the Nativity scene dispute speak most specifically to the ruling and its effects on the role of religion in politics in Rhode Island. Stephen Brown, Dennis Lynch, and Judge Pettine spoke openly to the press and to the author about how they received the news that the Court had sided with Pawtucket. Because each of their roles in the case was unique, their postdecision comments provide varied perspectives on the decision and its long-term significance.

Dennis M. Lynch

Dennis Lynch, the city official who became the major defendant in the suit and the city's leading spokesman, was gratified that his efforts as mayor and later as chairman of Citizens Committed to Continuing Christmas were successful. Most important for the former mayor was that the Court's decision appeared to endorse his belief that the majority had rights under the First Amendment. Even though in court the case was argued on Establishment grounds, the mayor and many of his constituents appeared to argue from the perspective that the issue raised important free exercise questions as well. Lynch said the ruling "restores faith in what this country is all about, freedom of its people to carry out its heritage and freedom."

The former mayor summarized the significance of the case with the following statement.[7]

> I think that the significance of *Lynch v. Donnelly* is the decision itself. The case was the first of its kind to get to the Supreme Court. And the Court heard it and ruled clearly. However, it seems that some people on both sides of the issue misinterpret what the Court said. The mentality of those who lost tends to downplay its importance for obvious reasons. Conversely, some who agree with our position tend to take the decision as one which solved all of the questions in this area of controversy. Neither position is correct.
>
> *Lynch v. Donnelly* restores and clarifies the rights of a community to carry on or establish its traditions and have public displays and celebrations of such national holidays as Christmas. The Court sustained that right so long as a Nativity Scene was part of the overall community display or celebration. If this condition was met, there was no establishment of religion violation.

The case also pointed out, it seems to me, that sensitivity to someone's feelings is, in fact, a two-way street. The community as a whole has a right to expect people to be tolerant of and sensitive to their collective feelings expressed publicly and legally.

Lynch declined to think that the Court ruling was any less significant because its vote was divided. "We won. When the New York Yankees win the World Series four games to three, I don't hear anyone telling them that they didn't win," he said.[8]

Not surprisingly, the individuals most closely aligned with the city's position tended to interpret the decision as a clear-cut endorsement of government's power to officially acknowledge the religious components of a community's heritage and traditions. What was important for them was that the majority sentiment had prevailed. Even though Lynch recognized that the Court limited its ruling to the specific facts that prevailed in Pawtucket, perhaps even his interpretation did not fully appreciate the complexity of the Court's approach to establishment of religion and the long-term impact of the city's thirty-nine-month controversy for questions relating to separation of church and state.

Stephen Brown

The impact of a Supreme Court ruling is more complex and involves other considerations than the actual decision itself. Although the Court decides for one side and against the other, it is possible in the long run to realize important gains in spite of having lost a court battle. The evidence from the impact of *Lynch v. Donnelly* in Rhode Island tends to support this view. Brown spoke to this point.[9]

I do feel all was not lost by the Supreme Court decision. First, on a national level, the Court's decision seems to have set, from the view of other courts and litigants, the outer boundaries of what is permissible under the First Amendment, and has not discouraged similar religious symbol suits from being filed and winning. The closeness of the Court's vote and the narrow concurring opinion of Justice O'Connor are perhaps largely responsible for that. Since the Pawtucket decision the Supreme Court has refused to review a lower court ruling striking down a government-sponsored creche that was not part of a larger secular display and two appeals court rulings striking down government displays of crosses. Thus, while I naturally remain concerned about the Pawtucket ruling, it at least appears to have been largely limited—explicitly by lower courts and implicitly by the Supreme Court—to its facts.

On a local level as well, the Court's decision ended up being far from a total loss. The educational importance of the lawsuit cannot be overstated. The suit created a healthy debate throughout Rhode Island on the meaning of the First Amendment and freedom of religion. The cumulative effect of this debate was an extremely positive one, as more and more people began to seriously consider and understand the principle for which the ACLU was fighting. This change in public opinion was obvious to me as the case progressed through the courts. In talk shows and in personal appearances I found more and more people supporting the ACLU's position every year.

I believe this change in opinion persisted even after the Supreme Court decision. Frankly, I had expected dozens of cities and towns to take the decision as a green light for the uncontrolled sponsorship of creches and other religious symbols. *But that did not occur.* Our educational mission appeared to have worked. Since the Supreme Court gave communities the legal right to sponsor creches, they now had to grapple directly with whether it was *appropriate* to do so, and most came down on our side. I am aware of no city or town that had not been sponsoring a Nativity Scene in the state that began doing so after the Pawtucket ruling was handed down. In fact, in at least one community a great controversy erupted when a private group sought permission to display a creche in front of town hall. Many residents objected, and the town council rejected the proposal. The number of voices raised against such a display simply would not have occurred prior to the Pawtucket case.

Let me give another example. Recently we filed a lawsuit challenging the display of a crucifix on public property in East Greenwich. Although there was a good deal of political posturing by town officials, we received virtually no hostile reaction whatsoever from the general public. And the suit is now on the verge of being settled out of court. I believe that this significant difference in reaction is attributable in large part to the positive educational aspects of the Pawtucket case. Rhode Islanders are much more sensitive to church–state issues than they were in 1980.

Of course, I cannot deny that the Pawtucket ruling was still a major setback and a retrenchment in the area of establishment of religion. At the same time, I have been pleasantly surprised at the positive after-effects our suit appears to have had.

One incident in December 1984 illustrates Brown's contention that the court challenge had changed some attitudes. In Providence, which had been a target of ACLU's Nativity scene efforts before the Pawtucket incident, Mayor Richard Paolino decided not to return the creche to City Hall steps. He noted that "the placement of any one religion's symbols on public property to express faith politicizes that faith and detracts from the sacred meaning those symbols hold." Even Bishop Gelineau endorsed the mayor's actions, noting that "it seems so improper to allow a symbol of peace and good will to become a source of division and controversy." [10]

Not all communities were spared from open hostility, however. When the Barrington town council denied a citizens' group permission to erect a manger scene, a public hearing "turned ugly as boos and hisses greeted those residents and members of the clergy who spoke out against returning the Nativity scene to the Town Hall front lawn." [11] It was this kind of public controversy that led Judge Pettine to speak out on the effect of the Supreme Court's ruling.

Judge Raymond J. Pettine

Judges rarely comment publicly on appellate reviews of their cases. However, in an unprecedented action, Judge Pettine used a forum on the separation of church and state at Temple Emanu-El in Providence on 26 October 1984 to comment upon the Supreme Court's reversal of his decision in *Lynch v. Donnelly*. In his remarks, which the *Providence Journal* described as an "eloquent tribute to the First Amendment," Judge Pettine discussed the delicate relationship that must exist between a judge's personal views and his responsibility as an officer of the court. That he felt compelled to speak from off the bench on the issue illustrates the case's consuming importance on the Rhode Island political agenda and also its pervasive impact upon Pettine and his conception of the First Amendment's religious provisions.

What follows is an edited compilation of Judge Pettine's remarks.[12]

I hesitate to comment on an appellate review of any of my cases. I never have. But the Nativity Scene case has caused such an eruption of emotion and I have been the target of such unimaginable vilification, that I feel free, now that the highest court has spoken, to do so.

In weak self-defense I like to point out that thirteen

judges heard *Lynch v. Donnelly* [Judge Pettine, three court of appeals judges, and nine Supreme Court justices]. If you add them up, you will see that seven said the city-sponsored Nativity Scene was unconstitutional and six found the practice constitutional.

More to the point, I found the Supreme Court decision offensive and its analysis of this question disturbing. By allowing the creche the Court has equated this holy symbol with tinsel, ornaments, reindeer, candy cane, and jolly old St. Nicholas. It seems the Court is willing to alter its analysis from term to term in order to suit its preferred result. There is no question government now faces the possibility of becoming involved in accommodating various demands of religious groups. There will be competing efforts by different religious sects to gain support of the government. In deciding to whom permission is to be granted, are we now going to allow government to decide what is and what is not a religion, who is or who is not entitled to equal courtesy? We can only pray that the Supreme Court ruling will not give rise to an insensitive profusion of government sponsored displays. I hope that government officials will act with restrained sensitivity.

The Constitution is a documental blessing and its moral guidance in the pluralistic society is its tolerance and understanding of all. To some non-believers the effect of the Court's decision is tacit coercion to accept the Christian faith. The appearance of government as sponsoring a religious view destroys the neutrality it should have. If we feel that others should be molded in the cause of our moral and religious thinking, the only weapon is teaching through debate without the imprimatur of government for one side or the other. If we fail to do this, history tells us that we may find, through change of circumstances, that we are no longer free in thought and worship because another sect has won the political rights.

I owe every respect to my confessor. Indeed in his role as such, he is monumentally awesome, and I subject myself to him. But as a citizen in the voting booth or a judge in the exercise of my duties, I respect all men, all religions, and listen objectively to the beliefs of others, divorced from my own personal convictions.

Certainly my personal religious morality has been contrary to some of the issues argued before me. As a judge, I am a public figure serving a pluralistic society. In such a role, I must consider, impartially and objectively, the convictions and beliefs of others. I speak from personal experience as a Catholic layman who is a federal judge in a democratic polity serving a heterogeneous mass of people. No God-fearing person wants to run counter to the didactic dogma of his faith, and that is good. But it seems to me God never intended that public officials, and voters, who conscientiously seek political justice, should dispense their public trust only for those who comport with their beliefs. Not unlike the kingdom of God, this Republic is open to all.

It is important to note that even after the dispute had concluded, each of the major participants remained true to the perspective that his particular role demanded. As the spokesman for the people of Pawtucket, Lynch was concerned that the majority be allowed to celebrate its tradition in the manner to which it was accustomed. In defeat, the ACLU stressed the fact that its goal to raise the level of awareness of Rhode Islanders concerning the feelings of the minority on sensitive church–state issues had been accomplished.

For Judge Pettine the issue was to clarify the law and to provide the necessary guidance to government officials who are sworn to perform their jobs and to administer government policy in accordance with the First Amendment. It is in this area that the case's long-term significance becomes most important. Many Court watchers would agree with Judge Pettine that the

Supreme Court's answer to the constitutional question raised in
Lynch v. Donnelly was deficient. The national debate that the
Nativity scene case set in motion illustrates this point.

THE NATIONAL RESPONSE TO
LYNCH V. DONNELLY

The Press

In the comment that opens this chapter, George Will expresses the view that the Supreme Court is all "mixed up" on the
establishment question. So, too, it can be argued, is the editorial
judgment of the nation's press. While it is not surprising to find a
lack of consensus among the members of the "fourth estate" on
government-supported Nativity scenes, the curious mix of opinion that was expressed belies the usually reliable conservative–liberal split in the press on most issues. If the Court has
difficulty finding unanimity on establishment issues, the press is
also "at sixes and sevens."

The conservative position on the Nativity scene issue is particularly divided. For example, contrast the attitudes of George
Will and James Kilpatrick on the creche. Will agrees that the
Court, in "rebelling against the tyranny of its own foolish for-
mulations and precedents," made the right decision. But he de-
nounces the way in which the Court arrived at its judgment.

> Burger also felt obliged to say, believe it or not, that
> Pawtucket's creche passes constitutional muster in part be-
> cause it has the secular purpose of abetting retail sales in
> downtown Pawtucket. And the Court's mania for splitting
> already-split hairs is visible [in the suggestion that] . . .
> there is significance in the fact that Pawtucket's Christian
> symbols were part of a tossed salad of seasonal symbols
> that included a reindeer, a sleigh, a Christmas tree, Santa's
> house, candy-striped poles, a teddy bear, an elephant, and a
> clown.

So the court, which is never more eloquent than when complaining about its workload, has incited more litigation which will come when the ACLU's beady eye spots a creche that might not have a constitutionally hygienic accompaniment of secular symbols.[13]

The appearance that Will is siding with Justice Brennan on the question of judicial standards on establishment is deceptive. In the end Will condemns the Court's reliance on the Lemon Test by arguing that Chief Justice Burger's seventeen-page opinion could have been reduced to a mere thirty-seven words if the justices had put the following sentence into their word processors: "Because the government practice at issue does not do what the Establishment Clause was written to prevent—does not impose a state-sponsored creed of significant advantage or disadvantage to one sect or sects—the practice is constitutionally benign."[14]

Kilpatrick takes a very different view. He argues that *Lynch v. Donnelly* was wrongly decided. A clear distinction between "God" and "Jesus" should be drawn. While all religions acknowledge a god, "the birth of Jesus, as described in the Christian Gospels, is an article of peculiarly Christian faith. For the government to spend public funds to erect a Nativity Scene strikes me as more than mere accommodation; it strikes me as an act respecting the establishment of religion. As such, it violates the supreme law of the land."[15]

Kilpatrick is not unsympathetic, however, to the concerns of those who believe that the Court has become too hostile to religion. When they deny children the opportunity to exercise their religious beliefs through voluntary prayer in schools, "the courts do wrongly," he argues.

The *Wall Street Journal,* probably the most conservative of the national newspapers, supported the decision but treated it less seriously than other representatives of the national press. Likening the case to a game of Trivial Pursuit, the *Journal* expressed surprise that a simple Nativity display could become a cause celebre. In noting the relationship of the courts to public opinion, its editorial concluded that the case "followed the hallowed court tradition of keeping one eye on the ballot box. If our friends are correct that its finding is unexceptionable, it suggests that the Court is in tune with the times."[16]

But not wishing to demean the importance of the difficult task of balancing religious commitment with religious tolerance, the *Journal's* editors expressed more concern with broader issues of church–state separation, such as the proposed constitutional amendment to legalize school prayers and with the oversecularization of public institutions and its impact on the breakdown of public morality.

The reaction of the political Left among the nation's press to the Nativity scene decision was more predictable. While they uniformly opposed the Court's ruling, their perceptions of its impact on the church–state question varied. One group saw the decision as a serious blow to religious liberty. The *Des Moines Register* found the majority's "contention that the danger of government imposition of an official religion or interference with the religious practice is less of a concern now than in the 18th century" to be "discouraging."[17] Nat Hentoff argued in the *Washington Post* that the publicly financed display of a symbol of a specific religious faith seriously eroded America's claim that it has no state religion.[18] In noting that Roger Williams established Rhode Island on the basis of a commitment to religious freedom, *Newsday* suggested "how ironic it is that the cradle of 'liberty in religious concernments' should also be its grave."[19]

The decision was less ominous to others on the liberal side. The *New York Times* found the manger scene "among the less troublesome forms of government interplay with religion." However, the Court's decision was still "deplorable" because it gave "the Court's constitutional blessing to the official use of a clearly sectarian symbol." While arguing that religious liberty would "survive the Court's approval of government-sponsored creches," the *Times* expressed the hope that the justices were "merely yielding on a legal fine point and [would] remain firm about more serious breaches of Government neutrality toward religion."[20]

Meg Greenfield of *Newsweek* includes herself among those "reluctant, unhappy, ambivalent souls who do not want to go around clearing the evidence of Christian exultation off every inch of public ground and yet who are also vaguely but persistently disturbed by the trend to introduce ever more elements of Christian liturgy into the practices of the state." In *Lynch v. Donnelly* the Court had breached the unspoken "compromise" that had existed on government use of religious symbols. "A punishing fight for principle is on. Each side feels it is being abused—one that it is being denied its religious consolation, the other that it is being told it doesn't belong. . . . This is one of those fights that can only make things worse no matter which side wins."[21]

The reaction of the national media to the Court's ruling in the Nativity scene case signaled a new stage in the public debate over the constitutionality of government acknowledgment of religious symbols and practices, and its impact on the larger question of the meaning of establishment of religion. Rather than tempering the controversy, the Court had energized the debate and raised the emotional stakes for those involved. This fact is no more clearly illustrated than by the reaction of the religious community to the *Lynch* decision.

The Religious Community

Throughout the courts' consideration of the Nativity scene question concern was raised about the actual and potential political divisiveness that resulted from government sponsorship of religious symbols. *Lynch* marked the first time the Court permitted the official display of a symbol that is explicitly and exclusively Christian. The ruling did little to calm the emotional debate that the controversy had created in religious circles. Reactions to the decision polarized the religious community. Roman Catholics and fundamentalist Christian groups applauded the ruling; Jewish and nonfundamentalist Protestant groups reacted angrily.

Jerry Falwell, leader of the fundamentalist Moral Majority, praised the decision by noting that there are worse things that occur on public property than the erection of Nativity scenes. For Falwell the decision represented a significant reversal of prior Court rulings. "It is most encouraging to observe the high court's recommitment to religious freedom in this country," he argued.[22] For the Moral Majority, a group that carefully monitors and publicizes its wins and losses, *Lynch v. Donnelly* was a victory.

The Roman Catholic hierarchy also endorsed the Court's opinion. The Conference of Catholic Bishops stated that the decision appeared "to affirm the reasonable view that government can accommodate the interest of its citizens in this matter without doing violence to any constitutional principle."[23]

The reactions of those who opposed the ruling were stated in more strident terms. The Reverend Dean Kelley of the National Council of Churches said the Court had "regressed from important principles of religious liberty by allowing government to sponsor religious symbols of one particular faith. The most sacred symbols of any faith should not be appropriated by the civil communities into being merely the emblems of 'a secular folk festival' on the same level as Santa Claus and Rudolph the Red-Nosed Reindeer."[24]

For most American Jews the decision's implications were more serious. Howard M. Squadron, president of the American Jewish Congress, argued that by expressly preferring Christianity over other religions, the Court created a situation in which the "American Jewish community is now a religious stranger in its own home."[25] Norman Redlich, dean of the New York University School of Law, explained the Jewish community's opposition to the Nativity ruling in an op-editorial essay in the *New York Times.*

> The United States Supreme Court's decision in the Pawtucket, R.I. creche case insults American Jews and all others who do not share what the Court's majority perceives as the country's dominant belief, Christianity. . . . While the Court's flagrant departure from the constitutional principle of church–state separation is, in this instance, particularly threatening to Jews, it should be equally troubling to members of all religious faiths. We are all partners in the American enterprise. What diminishes my freedom will ultimately diminish yours. . . .
>
> When I see a government-supported creche, I suddenly feel as if I have become a stranger in my own home, to be tolerated only as long as I accept dominant religious values. . . . The Constitution clearly rejects such an un-American, sectarian notion, and the Court should know better. . . .
>
> The experience of Jews worldwide adds to the profound significance of the Constitution's guarantee of religious neutrality. We have too long a history of living in countries where at best we were tolerated, at worst persecuted. In those countries, government-supported religious symbols have been the norm. Will we next be told that, as part of the secular observance of Easter, with eggs and bunnies, we should also accept the Crucifix as a simple recognition of an historical event?
>
> We cannot accept, or understand, the Supreme Court's insensitivity to our rightful place in American society. The Court's opinion, by seeking to "accommodate," does exactly what the Constitution was designed to prevent. It denigrates religion by trying to convert a religious symbol into a secular observance, and it shuts the door on those of

us who cannot accept a religious symbol because it conflicts with our deepest religious beliefs.

Jews should not be asked to accommodate. The most accommodating Jews in the contemporary history of the
Western world were the German Jews.[26]

If the intent of the First Amendment was to create a setting
in which all religious faiths could freely exercise their religious
beliefs without state interference, the divisions among the country's major religious sects created by *Lynch v. Donnelly* were
troubling. The implications for religious freedom and toleration
were also recognized by constitutional scholars.

The Legal Community Reaction

If judges value and heed the critical assessment of their work
by legal scholars, the Nativity scene majority can only conclude
that its efforts to clarify the meaning of establishment of religion
were unpersuasive. A common theme of the more than twenty-
five scholarly assessments of *Lynch v. Donnelly* in the nation's
leading law school reviews was that the Court had taken a back-
ward step.[27] The consensus was that what Justice Burger had
earlier perceived as an area "only dimly to be perceived" was
further clouded by the Pawtucket case. Phrases such as "confus-
ing," "unpersuasive," "wrongly concluded," "a misperception,"
and "a troublesome development" were used to describe the ruling and its long-term impact.

The opposition of the legal community to the *Lynch* decision was based on both substantive and procedural grounds.
Most legal scholars believed, first, that the decision was wrong
and, second, that the Court had done significant damage to the
principles it had devised to decide earlier cases. With its most
explicit endorsement of the power of government to acknowledge and accommodate religion, the Court had unwisely moved
away from the "strict interpretation" of establishment of reli-

gion agreed to by all nine justices in the 1947 *Everson* case. What was substituted was a kind of "philosophical seesawing" that made it impossible to know for sure what the Court meant by establishment or how it would look at future challenges.[28]

Particularly troubling to students of the law was that the decision significantly lowered the wall of separation between church and state and tended to encourage the kind of official government involvement with religion "feared by the Framers" and "intended to be prevented by the First Amendment."[29] The ruling sustained a practice that compromised the general neutrality of government. In choosing to finance the display of one religion's symbols, the government necessarily discriminated against other religions. One commentator noted that this new departure from tradition came just fourteen years after Chief Justice Burger had argued that the Framers were opposed to "sponsorship, financial support, and active involvement of the sovereign in religious activity."[30]

Specifically, the Court's legal critics accused the *Lynch* majority of ignoring the fact that a Christmas holiday display creates precisely the type of setting in which a creche would be perceived as government endorsement of religion in general, and of the Christian faith in particular. By allowing the religious majority in Pawtucket to use the machinery of the state to practice its beliefs, the Court chose to overlook the particularly Christian nature of the Nativity scene and the fact that it brought the religious content of the display to the forefront. Critics maintained that, for a holiday with both secular and sectarian elements, government's role should be limited to the secular parts of the holiday, not the affirmative encouragement of the religious aspects of Christmas' dual nature.[31]

More important to the Court's critics was the manner by which the majority reached its decision and the implications for future establishment cases. Justice Burger's reliance on historical precedent as one of the bases for deciding *Lynch* and the Court's erratic interpretation and application of the Lemon Test were seen by critics as likely to create confusion in the law. The message conveyed by the five-judge majority made it clear that it did not want to be confined to a single test in Establishment Clause cases. By abandoning the "relative certainty" of the Lemon Test, the Court appeared to opt for the "undefined territory" of a case-by-case analysis.

The assessment of the long-term impact of *Lynch* focuses in particular on the way in which the Court appeared to modify the tripartite Lemon Test. First, the ruling seemed to reject the notion that the challenged activity must exhibit a "clear" secular purpose. As a result of *Lynch,* government now needed only to show a "single" secular purpose. The modification created a "minimal burden," which, critics argue, virtually any government action promoting religion might be contrived to meet.[32]

The Court also failed to require government to show that its secular purpose could not be attained by other means. Testimony at the district court trial of witnesses for the city supported the position that Pawtucket could have accomplished its secular objectives without the Nativity scene. Furthermore, legal critics note that the Supreme Court ignored the district court finding that Mayor Lynch's goal was to "keep Christ in Christmas."[33] By not looking further into the actual intent of the display to determine whether there was a genuine secular purpose, the Court sent a signal that it would not actively examine or challenge government's stated purposes for entering into the area of religion.

Second, the *Lynch* decision is viewed as a retreat from the "separationist" effects of the second element of the tripartite test, that the primary effect of the government action must be neither to advance nor restrain religion. By arguing that "in each [establishment] case, the inquiry calls for line drawing; no fixed, per se rule can be framed," the Court maximized its own discretion to shape the results in individual cases. Rather than determine the "main" or "primary" effect of the Nativity scene, the *Lynch* Court effectively modified the test to permit more government support of religious activity by evaluating the practice from the perspective of whether it "confer[red] a *substantial* benefit" on religion.[34] Legal critics argue that as a result of *Lynch v. Donnelly* a practice whose primary purpose is religious, but whose benefit to religion is not substantial, now has a much greater chance to withstand an Establishment Clause challenge.

Finally, legal scholars contend that the Court significantly undermined the "entanglement" part of the Lemon Test by weakening the "divisiveness" part of the standard. By ruling that political divisiveness cannot alone "serve to invalidate otherwise permissible conduct," Justice Burger in effect has said that other grounds must be found to strike down government action.[35]

The concern of the professional critics of the Court is that the effect of its shifting position on *Lemon* will muddle the establishment issue on all fronts. Lower court judges will be uncertain how to apply the less-principled guidelines. Different courts will continue to rule differently in similar cases because no consensus exists as to when a religious activity becomes secularized or when the activity confers a "substantial" rather than an "indirect, remote, or incidental" benefit on religion. Reliance on historical precedent ignores the need to develop principles to deal with difficult establishment problems. Absent a principled basis on which to decide, intuition and the status quo become the acceptable judicial standards.[36]

The decision gives little guidance to towns seeking to avoid Establishment Clause problems. It may lead some municipalities to sponsor essentially religious displays amid "secular" disguises. Religious groups are encouraged to jockey for a favored position in the eyes of government. Official response to the competition among religious groups for public favor promotes divisiveness and increases government entanglement with religion. Legal scholars worry that, by tolerating practices that the jus-

THE REACTION / 178

tices perceived to be "mere shadows," the Court's shift away from "separationism" to "accommodation" will eventually create a "real threat" to the principle of separation of church and state not unlike what the Framers feared when they drafted the Bill of Rights.[37]

POST-*LYNCH* COURT ACTIVITY

Nativity Scenes

The Supreme Court's first effort to resolve the constitutionality of the Nativity scene had two major effects. First, the Court's decision was relied upon by others in government for guidance in complying with the law. The federal government cited the ruling in *Lynch* as the reason for returning a manger scene to the Christmas Pageant of Peace, a government-sponsored holiday display on the Ellipse, south of the White House. Some communities attempted to secularize their displays with nonreligious symbols or by posting disclaimers indicating that public funds were not being used. Other communities moved their displays from public property to avoid legal challenges.

More significant, however, is the fact that the *Lynch* decision occasioned a dramatic increase in litigation over public use of the creche and other religious symbols, such as the cross. Thus rather than settle the law in this controversial area, the Court provoked an extraordinary number of cases that raised questions that the *Lynch* decision had anticipated but left unanswered.

Just six months after *Lynch,* the Supreme Court agreed to hear another case involving a Nativity scene. In Scarsdale, New York, residents looked to the federal courts to overturn a decision of the village board that denied the application of two private groups to place a creche in a city-owned park for two weeks during the Christmas season. After permitting the Nativity scene for twenty-four years, the board in 1981 gave in to the growing number of protests and stopped the practice.

The New York case differed from *Lynch* in several respects. In Pawtucket the creche was displayed on private property; the Scarsdale creche was owned by private groups seeking to display it in a public park. Unlike in Pawtucket, where the Nativity scene was part of a larger display, in Scarsdale it stood alone. Plaintiffs contended that Scarsdale's actions denied them their constitutional rights of freedom of speech and free exercise of religion. Thus the question for the courts was whether a city that chooses not to display a Nativity scene on public property may be required by the Constitution to accede to the requests of groups who seek permission to do so.

The federal district court of New York, which ruled on the question before the Supreme Court's decision in *Lynch*, held that the exclusion of the creche was proper because of its purely religious nature and the state's compelling interest in avoiding conflict with the Establishment Clause.[38] However, with *Lynch* to guide its deliberations, the court of appeals reversed.[39] The court noted that the city-owned creche in Pawtucket was not construed as a primary advancement of religion. If a city by itself may erect a creche, then how can the Establishment Clause be violated by a private group doing the same thing? Scarsdale was merely accommodating a privately owned creche in a public park that is a traditional public forum. There was no active involvement, sponsorship, or financial support by Scarsdale.

McCreary v. Stone presented the Supreme Court with the opportunity to clarify its position on the public display of religious symbols and to answer some of the questions raised by the decision in *Lynch*. However, the decision resulted in more confusion. With Justice Powell not participating in the decision because surgery prevented him from hearing oral arguments, the Court divided 4–4.[40] A tie vote has the effect of affirming the judgment of the court below, but it has no precedential value in other cases. No written opinion accompanied the decision, and the Court did not identify the votes of the eight justices who participated. Scarsdale's creche was permissible, but the lower courts still had no clear signal on either Nativity scenes or other religious symbols.

The confusion that resulted from the *Lynch* and *McCreary* decisions in the lower courts is illustrated by three other challenges to the public display of the Nativity scene. In Birmingham, Michigan, the city's Christmas display was limited to a city-owned creche on the front lawn of City Hall. On 24 July 1984, four months after the Pawtucket decision, a federal district court judge ruled that the Birmingham creche was unconstitutional because it promoted only one set of religious beliefs.[41] The district court took a restrictive view of the *Lynch* decision by emphasizing the inclusion of the Pawtucket creche within the larger display in contrast to the "unadorned" creche in Birmingham.

The new Scarsdale decision did not help the court of appeals with the Birmingham case. In a 2–1 decision the appeals court affirmed the lower court view that Birmingham's display was a violation of the Establishment Clause. A creche standing alone has no significance or message other than that the birth of Jesus was an act of divine intervention.[42] It is the universally recognized symbol for the affirmation of Christianity and in the Birmingham context is an unconstitutional endorsement of a particular religion.

On 3 November 1986, the Supreme Court refused to review the Birmingham case. The effect of the denial of certiorari is to let the lower court decision stand. It does not necessarily mean, however, that the Court subscribes to the decision. It may simply mean that in a difficult area of constitutional law the Court prefers to wait for another opportunity to develop its position.

In Chicago, the creche was displayed in City Hall during the holiday season along with other secular elements of the season. In response to a suit filed by the American Jewish Congress, the district court held that, pursuant to *Lynch v. Donnelly*, the display was constitutional. However, on appeal, the Seventh Circuit Court of Appeals, in a 2–1 decision, reversed.[43]

The appeals court found that despite the display of non-religious holiday items throughout the building, the Nativity scene was a distinct exhibit that communicated the strong impression that the city tacitly endorsed Christianity. The fact that the display was located within a public building, a setting in which the presence of government is pervasive, and not, as in Pawtucket, in a privately owned park, also was a distinguishing factor for the court.

The occasion for the next Supreme Court consideration of the Christmas display question was announced on 3 October 1988, when it agreed to review a dispute arising from the city of Pittsburgh's placement of a creche inside the Allegheny County Courthouse and an eighteen-foot menorah on the front steps of the city–county building. The district court, relying on *Lynch*, refused to order the dismantling of the displays. However, the Third Circuit Court of Appeals ruled, by a 2–1 vote, that the displays unlawfully promoted religion. The majority argued that "the only reasonable conclusion is that by permitting the creche and the menorah to be placed at the buildings the city and county have tacitly endorsed Christianity and Judaism and have therefore acted to advance religion."[44]

The specific questions presented by the case are

(1) Does the county's display of a privately owned Nativity scene inside the county courthouse as part of its annual celebration of the Christmas holiday violate the Establishment Clause?

(2) Does the Establishment Clause prevent a municipality from placing, at no taxpayer expense, a Jewish symbol in its seasonal display?

(3) Is a municipality that erects a seasonal display that includes Christian symbols required by the Establishment Clause's prohibition against denominational preferences to permit the inclusion of a privately funded Jewish symbol?

The new case will be important not only for its result, but because it will be the first opportunity for Justice Kennedy, who replaced Justice Powell in the spring of 1988, to consider the constitutional relationship between government and religion. If Kennedy's views on establishment are more clearly defined than Justice Powell's, or if the Court uses the case to make dramatic changes in the test to be applied in freedom-of-religion cases, the result may, more than *Lynch v. Donnelly*, significantly advance the cause of those who believe that the First Amendment should allow government accommodation of religion. The possibility also exists that if the Court affirms the court of appeals ruling, that Stephen Brown was correct that *Lynch* represented the "outermost limits" permitted by the First Amendment as far as the public display of religious symbols is concerned.

The case was argued in the Supreme Court on February 22, 1989. At this writing, a June 1989 decision was expected.[45]

Crosses

The constitutionality of public displays of the cross has created the same mixed results and unpredictability in the lower courts as the creche. In applying the *Lemon* standards, the courts on some occasions sustained "public crosses" when a secular purpose could be identified. If a secular purpose was lacking, the cross was most often prohibited. Two decisions in the Oregon Supreme Court illustrate the principle. The erection of a cross in a municipal park was initially ruled to serve an impermissible religious purpose when it was lighted at Christmas and Easter. However, when the city approved a charter amendment accepting the cross as a memorial to U.S. war veterans, the court reversed its earlier decision on the grounds that the cross served a primarily secular function in the context of a war memorial.[46]

The Supreme Court was aware that parallels existed between the Nativity scene and the cross. On two occasions during the oral argument in *Lynch* the conversation turned to the question of the cross. In speculating on whether the city could display a cross for the celebration of Easter, attorney MacMahon conceded that "the association of a cross with a specifically religious holiday might well implicate the promotion of religion." However, he concluded that like the creche, "the cross and the star of David have legitimate secular uses depending on the context." ACLU attorney DeLuca attempted to undercut the city's position on "context" by asking the justices, "Why not display Easter bunnies and painted eggs and tulips, which are indicative or represent the secularization of Easter, along with the erection of a crucifix, since the crucifix is the real reason why Easter is being celebrated?"

The confusion that resulted from the uncertainty of the *Lynch* decision was evident from a Texas case in which the erection of three Latin crosses and a Star of David as part of a war memorial and place of meditation was challenged. The district judge ruled, "Because of recent aberrations from the Supreme Court's application of the traditional *Lemon* test, this Court's task is further complicated. The random approach by the Court to its analysis of Establishment Clause cases impels this Court to analyze . . . this case under all three tests . . . thought to be employed by that Court." After applying the Lemon, historical analysis, and strict scrutiny tests, the judge found Establishment Clause violations from each method of analysis.[47]

Although the Supreme Court has yet to consider a case in which the public display of the cross has been challenged, the lower courts have used the *Lynch* decision to distinguish between the cross and the Nativity scene. In three separate federal court decisions, public displays of the cross have been prohibited. In 1985, a lighted cross atop the Cos Cob, Connecticut, firehouse was struck down because it gave the appearance of governmental endorsement of a particular religion.[48] A year later the federal district court in Jackson, Mississippi, ordered that a twenty-story lighted cross on a state building be dismantled. The judge specifically noted, "The fact that the state has added nonsecular symbols does not make it constitutional."[49]

On 6 June 1986, Judge Richard Posner of the Seventh Circuit Court of Appeals issued an opinion that took a narrow view of the *Lynch* precedent. The issue was whether a lighted cross on the St. Charles, Illinois, firehouse was an unconstitutional mingling of church and state or simply a holiday decoration permissible under the standards set down in the Pawtucket case. In what some observers considered a significant slight to Supreme Court precedent, Posner found *Lynch* not applicable, noting that while some religious symbols may have lost part of their religious message, "the Latin cross has not lost its Christian identity." The public display of the cross "dramatically conveys" state support of Christianity. In contrasting the Illinois case with Pawtucket, Posner concluded, "The cross is understood to signify public support for Christianity rather than celebration of Christmas. The amount of support may not be great, but it is greater than in *Lynch*."[50]

In his first written opinion in an Establishment Clause case in 1970, Chief Justice Burger said of the Court's actions, "We have been able to chart a course that preserved the autonomy and freedom of religious bodies while avoiding any semblance of established religion. This is a 'tight rope' and one we have successfully traversed."[51] Many students of the Court see *Lynch v. Donnelly* as a major fall off that tightrope.[52] By appearing to take the position that the majority of Americans would not accept a complete prohibition against government accommodation of religion, the Court, rather than adhere to a principled approach to establishment of religion, chose to take on the task of "zigzagging" its way through the myriad cases that resulted from its own political pragmatism.

The concluding chapter examines this interpretation of the Nativity scene decision's significance from the larger perspective of the role of the courts in the political process and the principles the Court might have adopted to more effectively administer the Establishment Clause.

THE ESTABLISHMENT CLAUSE
REVISITED

> The three-part [Lemon] test has simply not provided adequate
> standards for Establishment Clause cases, as this Court has
> slowly come to realize. Even worse, [it] has caused this Court
> to fracture into unworkable plurality opinions. . . . The re-
> sults show the difficulty we have encountered in making the
> Lemon test yield principled results.
>
> Justice William Rehnquist

I T IS DIFFICULT TO FIND ANYONE who is willing to come to the
defense of the Supreme Court's record on questions of establishment of religion. The task is not an easy one. The variety of
religious views that are represented in the United States and the
sensitive nature of church–state relationships place an unusually
heavy burden on the courts. The justices themselves are aware
that their efforts have failed to produce agreement on a set of
principles to guide their consideration of the difficult constitutional questions raised by the "no establishment" provision.

Especially troublesome about recent Court decisions is that
new decisions regularly produce subtle, often unpredictable shifts
in position. The case-by-case approach to establishment has led
some observers to conclude that the tests the Court has devised

to make the clause operative play a deceptively limited role in the decision-making process. More important may be the particular results sought by the individual justices. Mark DeWolfe Howe, one of the earliest critics of the Court, echoed this sentiment by noting that on church–state issues it "has too often pretended that the dictates of the nation's history, rather than the mandates of its own will, compelled a particular decision."[1]

Unfortunately for the Court, however, looking into the "dictates of the nation's history" does not solve their problem. The scholarly debate over the Court's establishment decisions have produced two perspectives whose proponents disagree first on what history says about religion–government relations, and second on the role that it should play in deciding the disputes that arise today.

The Nativity scene decision only aggravated the controversy. The Court's rather vague references to history, its wavering commitment to the Lemon Test, and the continuation of a trend in which 5–4 splits were the norm did little to instill confidence in those judges and elected officials who rely on the Court for guidance that the meaning of Establishment had been clarified.

The critical assessment of *Lynch v. Donnelly* and its impact upon establishment law that follows explores two major themes. The first line of inquiry relates to a broader concern about the judicial process in American politics. What does the Nativity scene case tell us about the Court's unique role in our political system and the methods used by the justices to resolve constitutional disputes? The emphasis here is concerned with the ongoing debate over the appropriateness of the "historical record of original intent" as a standard for judicial decision making. The lack of consensus among judges about the role of the judiciary and the criteria that are relevant to its decisions is a major factor explaining the "unworkable plurality opinions" produced by the establishment controversies to which Chief Justice Rehnquist referred in the quotation that opens this chapter.

The second question relates to the specific decision in *Lynch*. Was it correct? Is there a way for citizens to publicly acknowledge and celebrate their religious heritage without offending the First Amendment? Would another approach to establishment questions better serve the needs of society and facilitate the courts' difficult task?

STANDARDS FOR JUDICIAL DECISION MAKING AND THE ESTABLISHMENT CLAUSE

Although court scholars and observers have argued about the scope of judicial power since the country's inception, the debate appears to have reached a new level of intensity in the 1980s. In part a reaction to the expansion of civil rights protections during the Warren Court era, conservative judges, scholars, and politicians have attacked a court system they believe to be dominated by judges bent on imposing their own personal views on the Constitution.[2] Too often, they allege, judges assume the role of "policy makers," preempting the decision-making responsibility of the Congress and of state legislatures. The Reagan administration, which is sympathetic to this view, has made a special effort to appoint judges who bring a more "traditional" approach to the bench; that is, an understanding that the role of the Court is to interpret law, not to make it.

This "traditional" perspective holds that any logical theory of constitutional interpretation must be derived from values found or implied in the text of the Constitution, in the intentions of the Framers, or in the "historical understandings" that have guided its implementation. The term used to describe this approach to judicial decision making is "interpretivism." The desired effect is to limit the Court's discretion and curtail the power of the judiciary vis-à-vis the elected branches of government.

The nontraditional perspective, noninterpretivism, maintains that "original intention" cannot be the only appropriate method of constitutional adjudication. Because evidence of the

Framers' intentions is sparse, ambiguous, and often contradictory, a judge must often look to evolving moral and ethical standards, which transcend the history surrounding the Constitution's adoption.[3] Many of today's problems were not envisioned
by the Framers. Neither did they contemplate a society as per-
vasively regulated by government as the United States is today.
Noninterpretivists believe that the interaction between judge
and constitutional text must be conditioned by an awareness of
social change and an understanding of contemporary values.

The Supreme Court's consideration of church–state issues
has provided ammunition for both sides on the "jurisprudence-
of-original-intention" dispute. Much of the argument that but-
tresses the "strict separationist–accommodationist" split on
establishment questions parallels this debate. The accommodationist perspective that prevailed in *Lynch v. Donnelly* rejected
the view that it was the intent of the Framers to create a complete and permanent separation of church and state. Chief Justice Burger's opinion for the Court argued that "such hostility
would bring us into war with our national tradition as embodied
in the First Amendment's guaranty of the free exercise of religion."[4] Separationists, on the other hand, not only question this
reading of the Framers' intent, but maintain that "it is unfair to
succeeding generations to turn a blind eye to social progress and
eschew adaptation of overarching principles to changes of social
circumstances."[5]

History and the Accommodationists

Accommodationists believe that much of the constitutional
law that governs church–state relations is wrong because the
Court has both ignored and misconstrued history. They are especially troubled by the "shocking" fact that virtually every
member of the *Everson* Court in 1947 endorsed a sweeping theory of strict separation.[6] Robert Cord, the author of the most
comprehensive accommodationist analysis, argues that many of
the Court's establishment rulings are akin to "fiction, completely

at odds . . . with the clear testimony of the primary historical documents and recorded events of American history."[7]

The critics of strict separation argue that a full examination of the historical record shows that the First Amendment was never meant to provide an "absolute" separation of church and state. All it was intended to do was to prevent the establishment of a national church or the conferring of a preferred status on any religious sect or denomination. Government aid to religion, when it was provided on a nondiscriminatory basis, was entirely permissible. According to accommodationists, the consequences of the Court's error in judgment is that churches today are too often excluded from participating in government programs that attempt to benefit the public by strengthening private sector institutions.[8]

Because they believe the separationist argument hinges largely on a faulty interpretation of the actions of James Madison and Thomas Jefferson, the traditionalists, in an effort to prove their point, reconstruct the historical arguments "to correct the record."[9] Their contention is that the actions of both presidents, who they argue were in positions that gave them considerable authority in the matter, provide a factual view of the Framers' intentions that is quite different from the "pseudoscholarly" analysis of strict separation.

They observe, for example, that James Madison was comfortable issuing Thanksgiving Day proclamations because they neither established a church nor preferred one religion over another. He also supported public prayer by a government-paid congressional chaplain. Jefferson provided land grants as inducements to missionaries to aid the Christian Indians, and signed a treaty that provided public funds to build a Catholic church. These and other historical illustrations in which government acknowledges America's religious traditions prove that an excessively broad interpretation of the First Amendment requiring a virtually absolute separation of church and state is historically incorrect and unsupportable.[10]

The interpretivist–accommodationist scholarship on establishment law attracted wide support from officials in the Reagan administration. Attorney General Edwin Meese publicly called for a return to a "jurisprudence of original intention" and challenged the Court to apply those theories to questions of separation of church and state. Rehnquist, Reagan's choice to succeed Burger as chief justice, repeated the essence of the historical reinterpretation of Madison and Jefferson in a 1985 dissenting opinion. He noted that the Court's effort to provide a clear test of the meaning of Establishment in *Lemon* "has no more grounding in the history of the First Amendment than does the wall theory upon which it rests. The three-part test represents a determined effort to craft a workable rule from an historical faulty doctrine." [11]

It is significant that the majority opinion in *Lynch v. Donnelly* was largely buttressed by the view that history supported the kind of government accommodation and acknowledgment of religion practiced in Pawtucket. Interpretivists were encouraged by the Court's adoption of a broad view of religion's role in our history to sustain the city's right to display the creche.

The Separationist Perspective on History

Separationists' contention that the state must provide no financial aid or symbolic support for religion is also based in part on a reading of history. Thomas Jefferson's "Virginia Bill for Religious Liberty" and his call for a "wall of separation between church and state" are extensively cited, as is Madison's opposition to "religious assessments." Even a proreligious justification for strict separation is found in Roger Williams' writings, which seek to preserve the church against the corrupting influence of the state. The fact that Congress at one point in the debates over the First Amendment passed a motion that said that Congress shall make no law "touching religion" is also offered as evidence that the intention of the Framers went well beyond the narrow interpretation of the accommodationists. [12]

Leonard Levy, one of the foremost separationist scholars, argues that one of the implications of the narrow historical interpretation of Establishment, that it permits aid and support to religion in general and when it is applied in a nondiscriminatory manner, has the effect of giving government more power than the Framers intended. The First Amendment was designed to restrict rather than enhance government power. "It is therefore unreasonable, even fatuous to believe that an express prohibition of power . . . vests or creates the power previously nonexistent, of supporting religion by aid to all religious groups." [13]

The broader view of the origins of the Establishment Clause goes on to argue, however, that when judges act solely as constitutional historians in seeking legal guidance, the results are often contradictory and other equally relevant factors in the decision-making process are neglected. Although he finds considerable support in the historical record for strict separation, Levy cautions that historical evidence never permits complete certainty. The Establishment Clause is sufficiently ambiguous in language and history to allow few sure generalizations.

> Anyone employing evidence responsibly should refrain
> from asserting with conviction that he knows for certain
> the original meaning and purpose of the Establishment
> Clause. The framers and the people of the United States . . .
> probably did not share a single understanding. A scholar or
> judge who presents his interpretation as the one and only
> historical truth . . . deludes himself and his readers.[14]

Relying exclusively on a historical approach to establishment also overlooks the changing nature of religion in American society. Justice Brennan warns of the dangers of treating the Constitution as a static document whose meaning is forever fixed by its founders.

> The inherent adaptability of the Constitution and its
> amendments is particularly important with respect to the

Establishment Clause. Our religious composition makes us a vastly more diverse people than were our forefathers. In the face of such profound changes, practices which may have been objectionable to no one in the time of Jefferson and Madison may today be highly offensive to many persons, the deeply devout and the nonbeliever alike.[15]

Justice Brennan noted in his *Lynch* dissent that "the American historical experience concerning the public celebration of Christmas provides no support for the Court's decision."[16] At the time of the Constitution's adoption there was no settled pattern of celebrating Christmas. The historical evidence suggests that the development of Christmas as a public holiday and the display of the Nativity scene are comparatively recent phenomena.

However, even if the evidence existed, Brennan would not put the Court in a historical straightjacket. It matters not that in the context of the eighteenth century Nativity scenes or legislative chaplains may have seemed appropriate within the spirit of the First Amendment. The religious diversity of today may sometimes require a different interpretation of the Establishment Clause to promote the same values the Founding Fathers first sought to protect.

The decision in *Lynch v. Donnelly* clearly manifests both the separationist–accommodationist split on establishment and the larger controversy over the role of original intention. The majority finds support for their view that the history is pervaded by official acknowledgment of the role of religion in American life. The dissent discerns no historical precedent for the practice of publicly sponsored Nativity scenes and is careful to note that even if examples could be found, "no one acquires a vested or protected right in violation of the Constitution by long use, even when that span of time covers our entire national existence and indeed predates it."[17]

Thus the justices are no more in agreement about history than they are over the meaning of the Lemon Test. In restating Mark Howe's earlier observation, Richard Jones demonstrates that "different judges weigh historical facts differently and apply the same neutral tests differently." He concludes that "the outcome of cases at the Supreme Court level cannot be predicted by focusing upon the test alone. To predict how the Court will act on a particular issue, the focus of attention should be placed on the broader, underlying perspective of each individual justice on the Court at the time." [18] What often appears to be a kind of "result oriented" jurisprudence in establishment cases is an imposing target for critics of the Court looking for a foundation based on principle. Guiding principles have been difficult to come by. Many scholars subscribe to the view that First Amendment religion law remains in a state of chaos.

Perhaps the best that can be said for the Court is that it has followed a pragmatic approach to establishment cases, which generally leaves it in the space between the extremes of the accommodationist and the separationist positions. In attempting to foster a policy which Chief Justice Burger called "benevolent neutrality," the Court has opted to remain flexible and to rethink or modify its decisions on a case-by-case basis. Not unlike the legislation produced by Congress, judicial decisions are also a product of compromise influenced by the particular mix of competing views represented by the nine justices at any given time.

THE COURT'S APPROACH TO ESTABLISHMENT: EVALUATION AND ALTERNATIVES

An argument can be made that the most important function of the Supreme Court is to ensure that the actions of the lower courts and political branches of our government conform to the meaning of the Constitution. The decisions of the High Court should provide a degree of certainty about the law. Their effect should be to reduce controversy and lighten the judicial caseload.

When viewed from this perspective it is often argued that the Court's approach to establishment of religion has failed. Individually the justices' views span a wide ideological spectrum. Collectively their opinions have attempted to fashion a compromise that has confused the issue more than clarified it. The effect of the Court's decisions has been to increase rather than reduce the judicial caseload. Church–state issues have been raised to a more prominent place on the political agenda.

The Nativity scene decision aptly illustrates the lack of clarity and confusion that has resulted from virtually all of the Court's rulings that attempt to accommodate religion within the meaning of the Establishment Clause. As a result of *Lynch* the courts must, on a case-by-case basis, sort through a series of imponderable variables to determine whether the display of a creche has the effect of advancing or endorsing religion. Relevant to the decision are (1) the location of the display, (2) whether it is part of a larger holiday setting that includes nonreligious items, (3) the intensity of the religious message, (4) whether the creche is displayed in conjunction with a general secular holiday, (5) the degree of government involvement in the ownership and maintenance of the display, and (6) the existence of any disclaimer of government sponsorship.

With *Lynch* as precedent, the lower courts have had to contend with an increasing number of Nativity scene suits in which groups on both sides of the issue seek to maneuver the Court toward their own position. The application of the Court's standards has not been uniform. Holiday displays that seem very similar in purpose and effect often produce different decisions. Whether the *Lynch* decision is narrowly or broadly defined is often subject to the vagaries of an individual judge.

Should we expect more from the Court on this difficult constitutional question? If so, where did it go wrong? Would another legal approach have helped the Court to avoid the problems it has encountered in developing judicial standards to clarify the meaning of Establishment?

To answer these questions adequately is clearly beyond the scope of this case study. Another book would be required. However, to suggest the contours of the debate and to stimulate thinking about the church–state issue and the courts' role in the controversy, three different "answers" to these questions are suggested below. First is the position that defends the overall results achieved by the Court's balancing of the interests of separationists and accommodationists. Second is the view that the Court should modify and refine its standards for interpreting Establishment. Third is the argument that a more literal, "absolutist," reading of the Establishment Clause would better serve the Court.

In Defense of the Court

One of the problems to confront the modern Supreme Court is the widespread acceptance of a religious element in much of American public life. We pledge allegiance to "one nation, under God." Our coins and national motto proclaim "In God We Trust." The government legislates a National Day of Prayer, and our elected officials often resort to spiritual references in their public oratory. A recent public opinion survey revealed that Americans value freedom of religious worship as much as they do the freedom to vote.[19] Judeo-Christian religious beliefs are considered by a majority of citizens to be a positive force in shaping the values of a democratic society. A loss of religious faith is often associated with a permissiveness that tends to undermine both private and civic morality.

In an opinion that has received almost as much attention as Justice Black's *Everson* definition of establishment, Justice Douglas observed that "we are a religious people whose institutions presuppose a Supreme Being. . . . We find no constitutional requirement which makes it necessary for government to be hostile to religion or to throw its weight against efforts to widen the effective scope of religious influence."[20] Douglas' statement dramatizes the tension in Establishment Clause jurisprudence between a significant religious dimension in American political culture and the constitutionally suspect character of a number of time-honored public practices.

The Court is not unaware of the impact of its decisions on public opinion. The justices are sensitive to the fact that a strict separationist assault on those aspects of our public ritual and on rhetoric where the religious intersects with the political would not be popular. Justice Brennan's dissent on the Pawtucket Nativity scene controversy pointed out the dilemma. "I am convinced that this case appears hard not because the principles of decision are obscure, but because the Christmas holiday seems so familiar and agreeable."[21]

A persuasive case could be made that the Court has backed away from a principled challenge to many questionable church–state relationships because these have a long practice and seem to be so "familiar and agreeable" to most Americans. Also, the fact that in the late forties and early fifties the justices were operating in an international climate in which an atheistic brand of communism had surfaced as a major threat to democracy may have also influenced establishment decisions. In that context it became more difficult to argue that religious values could thrive and shape the moral climate of our society without the active support of government. The problem that persists for the Court is to find a way to enforce a strict separation of church and state in a culture that publicly acknowledges its religious heritage.

Some scholars believe that the Court's pragmatism on establishment questions has served the country well. They minimize the need for clear constitutional principles and point to the Court's role as an agent of political compromise. Morris Abram sums up the view of those who believe that the Court's failure to set down principles in its religion cases does not represent a serious flaw.

> Generally speaking, the Supreme Court, faced with the monumental task of drawing vague boundary lines, mapping the territories where the church and state should remain separate and where they should be permitted to overlap, has successfully reconciled the powerful social pressures and seemingly inconsistent values with which it has had to struggle. The results that the Court has reached, while clearly difficult to harmonize with a rigidly doctrinal perspective, have accommodated religious exercise without violating establishment.[22]

In a similar line of argument Philip Johnson asks that we judge the Court's performance not on the basis of its conceptual coherency, but as an exercise in political compromise that can be accepted by persons of widely differing religious views.

> The fact that constitutional doctrine is at times muddled and internally inconsistent does not necessarily mean that it is intolerable. On the contrary, the very fact that the holdings do not fit any abstract pattern may indicate that the Court is steering a careful path between undue preferences for religion or undue hostility to it. . . . A body of decisions that is meant to keep the peace between strong contending factions may seem incoherent to those who wrongly suppose that the Court's purpose is to put into effect some abstract doctrinal principles.[23]

Johnson goes on to argue that constitutional law regarding religion looks a good deal better from this perspective as an exercise in balancing competing interests. Separationists and accommodationists alike can claim that their causes have been advanced by the Court. *Lynch v. Donnelly* illustrates his point.

Accommodationists have been allowed to continue to include the Nativity scene in the Pawtucket Christmas display. Separationists, however, can take comfort in the fact that the vote was close and that the decision was justified on such narrow grounds. Neither the pure accommodationists nor the militant secularists win all the battles. Each side has reason to view the situation with at least partial satisfaction.

Another Approach to Establishment

Other students of the Court believe that the First Amendment's Free Exercise Clause might be more effectively used as a counterweight to Establishment. The same Constitution that mandates that the advancement of religion should not come from the political and financial support of the state also guarantees freedom of conscience and the right of all individuals to practice their beliefs free from government coercion or discrimination.

In many instances it is difficult to separate establishment from free exercise claims. Laurence Tribe has observed that "although cases are occasionally litigated under one clause or the other, . . . the interplay of the two clauses will almost always prove more decisive than either clause viewed in isolation."[24] His conclusion is that "whenever a free exercise claim conflicts with an absolute non-establishment theory, the support of the former would be more faithful to the consensus present at the time of the Constitutional Convention and of the First Congress."[25]

Justice Brennan also sees the Establishment and Free Exercise Clauses in a kind of reciprocal relationship. In the 1962 Bible-reading case he suggested the following constitutional standard for the religion clauses.

> Neither can Government give, either directly or indirectly, any aid, money, services, or support to any religion or any religious organization, nor can Government impose, directly or indirectly, any burden, tax, or regulation on any

religion, religious organization, or individual in the practice of his/her religion, unless such burden is required by a compelling state interest that can be achieved by no other means.[26]

Linking the two religious clauses and imposing a "no-aid, no-burden" constitutional standard would bring the Court closer to the principled approach sought by its critics. Had it rigorously applied such a standard to the Nativity scene case, the Court might have rejected Pawtucket's claim that its effort did not serve to aid or promote religion. In so doing it could also have pointed out that Christians who desire to celebrate the Nativity season in a public way still have Free Exercise rights to protect their religious freedom. None of the *Lynch* decisions prevented individuals or religious groups from displaying creches in front of their homes or on church property. It is also clear that under certain conditions municipalities retain the right to grant religious groups access to public property to express their beliefs.

For example, in its 1981 decision in *Widmar v. Vincent* the Court ruled that the University of Missouri could not discriminate against a student religious group by denying it access to university facilities that were open to other student groups. Justice Powell spoke for an 8–1 majority (Justice White dissenting) when he argued that "the Establishment Clause does not bar a policy of equal access in which facilities are open to groups and speakers of all kinds. . . . The Constitution forbids a state to enforce certain exclusions from a forum generally open to the public. . . . It does not follow that an 'equal access' policy would be inconsistent with the Court's Establishment Clause cases."[27]

Courts have also generally held that public parks are a traditional public forum and that religious groups have as much right to use them as nonreligious groups. So long as all groups, religious and nonreligious, are treated equally and each user complies with the rules set up for the use of the public facility, freedom of speech protects religious views as well as other forms of speech. Only if a religious display or some other form of activity on public property gives the appearance of governmental sponsorship does it become constitutionally suspect.

If the Court were to support the "public forum" approach as an alternative to using a municipally owned and tax-supported display to promote the religious aspects of the Christmas holiday, it would provide clearer constitutional standards that both separationists and accommodationists might be prepared to accept. A society that assiduously promotes the free exercise of religion has little to fear from a strict enforcement of separation of church and state.

A More "Absolute" Approach to Establishment

Hindsight suggests that in the very first significant establishment decision, *Everson v. Board of Education,* the Court went astray when it eschewed a principled decision-making approach. Had the Court fully embraced Justice Black's strict separationist view of Establishment and not "excepted" school bus transportation from its meaning, the result might well have led to a principled approach to questions of separation of church and state that would have spared the Court from having to strike what has turned out to be a highly illusive and politically divisive compromise.

Chief Justice Rehnquist provides some backhanded support for this view. He has observed that despite "the absence of an historical basis for the theory of rigid separation, the wall idea might well have served as a useful albeit misguided concept, had it led this Court to unified and principled results in Establishment Clause cases. The opposite unfortunately has been true; in the thirty-eight years since *Everson* our Establishment cases have been neither principled nor unified." [28]

Notwithstanding Rehnquist's contention that it lacked an historical basis, would it have been inappropriate for the Court in *Everson* to prohibit public subsidization of transportation to religious schools? The public school system, which did not evolve until the mid–nineteenth century in the United States, was based in part on the premise that secular education should be isolated from religious teaching. Educators believed that knowledge and values could and should be taught in a learning environment which maintained a strict neutrality as to religion. Those who persisted in their belief that the proximity of education to religious values should be maintained, could claim the protection of the Free Exercise Clause and opt for religious schools. It was the Court's duty, however, to uphold the equally important concerns of Establishment. In his dissenting opinion in *Everson*, Justice Robert H. Jackson stated:

> I should be very surprised if any Catholic would deny that the parochial school is a vital, if not the most vital, part of the Roman Catholic Church. Its growth and cohesion, discipline and loyalty, spring from its schools. Catholic education is the rock on which the whole structure rests, and to render tax aid to its Church School is indistinguishable to me from rendering the same aid to the Church itself. . . . The state cannot maintain a Church and it can no more tax its citizens to furnish free carriage to those who attend a Church.[29]

What was so remarkable about *Everson* was that all nine justices embraced the strict separationist stand that Justice Black had set down. None of the members of that Court, including justices who had eloquently defended the "conservative," or "self-restraintist," position, gave any hint of support for the accommodationists' arguments that surfaced in the 1980s. The legal community criticized *Everson* not for its definition of what constitutes establishment, but for the majority's abrupt and unpersuasive support for tax-supported bus transportation to parochial schools.

The *Everson* Court came close to providing the principled standard many look for from the Court. Only Justice Black's last-second reprieve for tax-supported money for parochial school transportation prevented a unanimous agreement that might have been a more effective and constitutional precedent. Black himself became alarmed when the Court used the school bus precedent to allow public support for textbooks to religious schools.[30] In subsequent cases where the justices resisted the view that changing circumstances can put old practices and the Constitution in a new light, the Court's attempt to fashion a publicly acceptable compromise has only muddied the constitutional waters and raised religious sensibilities on the public agenda, a situation the Founding Fathers sought to prevent.

What if the Court had ruled in 1947 that religion occupied such a special and unique place in American society that it was imperative that the words of the Constitution be taken literally and absolutely, that government could make *no* law respecting the establishment of religion? In the words of Justice Rutledge, speaking for the four dissenters in *Everson,* the purpose of the First Amendment was "to create a complete and permanent separation of religious activity and civil authority, comprehensively forbidding every form of public aid or support for religion. It outlaws all use of public funds for religious purposes."[31] Had this "no-aid" strict separationist view prevailed, bus transportation, textbooks, and even publicly supported Nativity scenes would have been nipped in the bud.

In his dissenting opinion in the legislative prayer case, Justice Brennan recalled a passage from Alexis de Tocqueville where he was attempting to explain the unique religious atmosphere he found in America during his travels in the 1830s.

> To find this out, I questioned the faithful of all communions; I particularly sought the society of clergymen, who are the depositaries of the various creeds and have personal

interest in their survival. I expressed my astonishment and revealed my doubts to each of them; I found that they all agreed with each other except about details; all thought that the main reason for the quiet sway of religion over the country was *the complete separation of church and state* [emphasis added]. I have no hesitation in stating that throughout my stay in America, I met nobody, lay or cleric, who did not agree about that.[32]

Brennan concluded that more recent history has only confirmed Tocqueville's observations. The justice speculated that if the Court had struck down legislative prayer, it would "have stimulated a furious reaction." He also observed that this would have also "invigorated both the spirit of religion, and the spirit of freedom."[33] The same argument could be made for the Court's Nativity scene decision.

In the short term, the strict separationist position on questions of separation of church and state may seem like a betrayal to much of American society and culture. In the long run, however, it may be the only method to guarantee that all individuals, believers and nonbelievers alike, are free to pursue their First Amendment rights. There is no necessary reason why government and religion must be involved in the other's domain. History tells us that the union of government and religion does more to disable societies than a strict enforcement of their separation. The public furor over the Pawtucket creche and the disarray that has resulted from government's attempts to accommodate religion within the public sector, provide another timely illustration that "as government acts more deeply upon those areas of our lives once marked 'private,' . . . the possibilities for collision between government activity and individual rights will increase. . . . There is an even greater need to see that individual rights are not curtailed or cheapened in the interest of what may temporarily appear to be the 'public good.'"[34]

CONCLUSION

Famed constitutional scholar Robert Cushman wrote in 1925 that "the Supreme Court does not do its work in a vacuum. Its decisions on important constitutional questions can be understood in their full significance only when viewed against the background of history, politics, economics, and personality surrounding them and out of which they grew."[35] Whether one agrees or disagrees with the court rulings on the public display of Nativity scenes, or whether one takes a separationist or accommodationist view of the Establishment Clause, it is clear from *Lynch v. Donnelly* that courts in the United States are integral agents in the development of public policy, operating well within the mainstream of the political process.

Constitutional provisions are written in broad language. The task of giving meaning to the phrase "respecting the establishment of religion" demands that the courts be something more than a "body of legal technicians above and beyond the political struggle." The answers to controversial judicial disputes are never easy. It was inevitable, when justices Burger and Brennan sat down to write their opinions on the constitutionality of Pawtucket's Nativity scene, that each judge, within the limits and authority of his office, would bring his own set of values to the task. The opinions in *Lynch* illustrate just how each judge utilized the resources of his position to achieve a very different set of policy objectives.

Thus judges, like legislators, are human beings prepared to intervene on behalf of values they prize. Judicial decisions, like statutes, help to shape public policy. This is not to say, however, that the judicial and legislative processes do not have their distinctive characteristics. We have observed that judges operate in an institutional context whose ethos is very different from that of legislators or administrators. The methods by which judges are selected and the formal and informal rules that govern their consideration of cases give them a different perspective on the issues with which they deal. Supreme Court judge Benjamin Cardozo eloquently spelled out the unique role of the judge in the following:

> The judge, even when he is free, is still not wholly free. He is not to innovate at pleasure. He is not a knight-errant roaming at will in pursuit of his own ideal of beauty or of goodness. He is to draw his inspiration from consecrated principles. He is not to yield to spasmodic sentiment, to vague and unregulated benevolence. He is to exercise a discretion informed by tradition, methodized by analogy, disciplined by system, and subordinated to the "primordial necessity or order in the social life."[36]

Not all students of the judiciary would agree with Cardozo, nor would they interpret his words in the same way. The fear is often expressed that some judges carry their involvement in policy making so far as to blot out any distinctive characteristics to the judicial process. However, there will always be disagreements about the position of the courts in American politics. Judges will come to the bench with differing conceptions of their role in the political system, driven by competing political attitudes and values. The story of *Lynch v. Donnelly* is evidence that the courts are more than impartial and disinterested observers in the political system, and that judicial policy making is not a form of deviant behavior, but an inevitable and proper function of the judiciary.

When it was asked to decide under what conditions the Constitution permits the public display of the Nativity scene, the courts had little choice but to become involved in a controversial political question. No matter what decision had been rendered, the judges would have been endorsing the values of one segment of society and opposing the views of others. Different courts came up with different answers. The results were pleasing to some, disappointing to others. The seasoned observer of American politics knew, however, that no single court case would put the Nativity scene question to rest. All important political questions in the United States tend to be recurring. All solutions tend to be interim. This even applies to questions that go to the heart of the Constitution, where federal judges have a special role.

LYNCH v. DONNELLY:
Case Chronology

____ 1980 _____

17 December   The Rhode Island affiliate of the American Civil Liberties Union, acting on behalf of Daniel Donnelly, a Pawtucket resident, files suit against the city in the U.S. district court in Providence. The complaint alleges that the Nativity scene in the city's Christmas display is in violation of the Establishment Clause of the First Amendment.

18 December   Mayor Dennis M. Lynch holds a press conference in front of the creche. He vows to fight the suit and leads the crowd in singing Christmas carols.

19 December   Chief Judge Raymond J. Pettine defers action on the suit until after Christmas. He indicates that the case raises serious constitutional questions which deserve a full hearing.

____ 1981 _____

3–6 February   Judge Pettine hears testimony in a fact-finding trial in district court.

30 August	Judge Pettine issues a tentative opinion warning that plaintiff Donnelly may lack the taxpayer's standing necessary to bring the suit.
18 September	The ACLU amends the suit by adding three Pawtucket taxpayers to the complaint.
10 November	*Judge Pettine rules that the city-sponsored Nativity scene violates the First Amendment ban on government promotion of religion.*
30 November	Judge Pettine denies Pawtucket's request for a stay, pending an appeal, of his order that the Nativity scene not be included in the city's Christmas display.
3 December	The city sells the Nativity scene to a private group.
5 December	The Citizens Committee, led by former mayor Lynch, installs the creche in Hodgson Park, in a space left vacant in the city-owned portion of the display.
9 December	ACLU attorneys request that Judge Pettine hold Pawtucket in contempt of court. They allege that the erection of the creche next to the city's display gives the appearance of government sponsorship.
10 December	Judge Pettine rejects the ACLU motion. Pawtucket files a motion with the U.S. Court of Appeals for the First District appealing the district court ruling and requests that the court of appeals postpone Judge Pettine's ban on the creche.
11 December	The court of appeals denies the city's request for a stay.

___ 1982 ___

7 April	The court of appeals hears arguments in the case.

3 November   *The court of appeals upholds the district court ruling in a 2−1 decision.*

—— 1983 ——

26 January   Pawtucket files a writ of certiorari to the U.S. Supreme Court requesting that it review the lower court decision.

18 April   The Supreme Court agrees to hear the case.

4 October   The Supreme Court hears oral arguments.

—— 1984 ——

5 March   *The Supreme Court, in a 5−4 decision, reverses lower court decisions, holding that the Nativity scene does not violate the Establishment Clause of the First Amendment.*

GLOSSARY

ACCOMMODATIONIST   An individual who believes that the Establishment Clause permits aid to religion if it is administered in a non-preferential manner. Same as *Nonpreferentialist.*

ACTIVIST   See *Judicial activist.*

AMERICAN BAR ASSOCIATION   A professional association of attorneys in the United States that screens federal judicial nominees for competence in the law.

AMERICAN CIVIL LIBERTIES UNION   A national organization devoted to the protection of individual rights and civil liberties.

AMICUS CURIUS   From the Latin meaning "friend of the court." It refers to an individual or organization that is not a party to a court case but that is interested in the result. The court grants permission to file a written brief to present the perspective of the amicus curius in a case.

APPEAL   The procedure by which a losing party takes its case to a higher court for review.

APPELLATE JURISDICTION   A case received from lower courts. Article III of the Constitution gives Congress the power to define the appellate jurisdiction of the Supreme Court.

ASSOCIATE JUSTICE   A judge of the Supreme Court or a lower court who is not a chief justice.

BRIEF   A written document prepared by attorneys to present their argument to a court.

CASE   A legal controversy to be decided by a court.

CERTIORARI   See *Writ of Certiorari*.

CHIEF JUSTICE   The presiding judge of the Supreme Court.

CIRCUIT COURTS   See *Courts of Appeals*.

CONCURRING OPINION   An opinion by a judge who agrees with the decision of the court but who chooses to express his or her own reasoning on the matter.

CONFERENCE   See *Judicial Conference*.

COURTS OF APPEALS   The general appellate courts for the federal judicial system. They review cases from the district courts and certain rulings of federal administrative agencies.

DEFENDANT   The party to a case against whom relief is sought.

DISSENTING OPINION   An opinion by a judge that expresses disagreement with the opinion of the court.

DISTRICT COURTS   The basic courts of original jurisdiction in the federal court system.

DUE PROCESS CLAUSE   The section of the Fourteenth Amendment to the Constitution that provides that states shall not deprive any person of life, liberty, or property without due process of law. Courts have used it to bring states into conformity with the Bill of Rights. See *Incorporation*.

ESTABLISHMENT CLAUSE   The clause in the First Amendment that has been interpreted to prohibit government support of religion.

EXCESSIVE ENTANGLEMENT   The portion of the Lemon Test guidelines for interpreting the Establishment Clause that makes unconstitutional activities involving government officials too closely in the affairs of religion.

FREE EXERCISE CLAUSE   The clause in the First Amendment that provides that government must guarantee religious freedom.

INCORPORATION   The process by which the Supreme Court has applied the protections of the Bill of Rights to actions of state and local governments through the Due Process Clause of the Fourteenth Amendment.

INTERPRETIVISM   The theory that the courts should interpret the constitution from the perspective of the intentions of the Framers and historical understanding.

JUDICIAL ACTIVIST   A judge who is more apt to strike down legislation when he or she believes it conflicts with contemporary understandings of the Constitution. He or she does not feel as bound to the literal words of the Constitution or the intention of the Framers as judges who follow judicial restraint.

JUDICIAL CONFERENCE   A closed meeting of the Supreme Court justices during which cases are discussed and voted upon.

JUDICIAL RESTRAINTIST   A judge who is reluctant to declare actions unconstitutional unless they clearly violate the words of the Constitution or the intention of the Framers. Opposite of *Judicial Activist*.

JUDICIAL REVIEW   The power of the courts to determine the constitutionality of statutes and actions of executive officials. It was first spelled out by Chief Justice John Marshall in *Marbury v. Madison* (1803).

LEMON TEST   The three-part test derived by the Supreme Court to evaluate challenges to the Establishment Clause. It provides that the challenged activity (1) must have a clear secular purpose; (2) must, in primary effect, neither advance nor retard religion; and (3) must not foster excessive governmental entanglement.

MAJORITY OPINION   The written statement by a Supreme Court justice that explains the Court's decision. Same as *Opinion of the Court*.

NONINTERPRETIVISM   The theory that the courts should not be limited to the literal words of the Constitution or the intentions of the Framers in making decisions. It allows judges to use evolving contemporary standards to decide cases.

NONPREFERENTIALIST   See *Accommodationist.*

OPINION OF THE COURT   See *Majority Opinion.*

ORAL ARGUMENT   The Supreme Court session in which attorneys present their arguments and the justices have the opportunity to question the litigants.

ORIGINAL JURISDICTION   The power of a court over cases that began in that court.

PLAINTIFF   The party that brings an action in a suit.

PLURALITY OPINION   The opinion of the Court in a case in which the majority is divided as to the reasoning to be applied to a decision. In some instances the opinion of the Court may not reflect the views of individual justices who voted with the majority. See *Concurring Opinion.*

POLITICAL QUESTION   A question that the Court refuses to decide because it believes it can be more appropriately addressed by elected officials.

RESPONDENT   In appellate jurisdiction, the party against whom the appeal is being made.

RULE OF FOUR   The practice of the Supreme Court to accept only those cases in which at least four of the justices are willing to grant certiorari.

SENATORIAL COURTESY   The custom in the Senate of rejecting a federal judicial nomination in a state if a senator or senators of the president's party find the nominee objectionable.

SOLICITOR GENERAL   The government's lawyer in the courts. The solicitor general argues the government's cases in the Supreme Court.

STANDING TO SUE   The plaintiff's showing that he or she has a substantial personal interest in a suit and that he or she has been injured or is in danger of injury from some action of the government.

STARE DECISIS   The courts' practice of giving substantial weight to precedents established in prior decisions.

STRICT SCRUTINY   A judicial standard in which the Court asks if the government has a compelling interest in administering a challenged law or policy.

STRICT SEPARATIONIST   A person who believes that separation of church and state should be strictly enforced. Opposite of *Accommodationist.*

SUPREME COURT   The court of last resort in the U.S. judicial system.

WALL OF SEPARATION   The term used first by Thomas Jefferson to describe his conception of the separation of church and state. It is used by strict separationists to support their beliefs.

WRIT OF CERTIORARI   A petition to the Supreme Court requesting that it hear a case.

TABLE OF CASES:
Supreme Court Establishment
Decisions (1947–1988)

Abington Township School District v. Schempp, 374 U.S. 203
  (1963)
Aguilar v. Felton, 473 U.S. 402 (1985)
Board of Education v. Allen, 392 U.S. 236 (1968)
Committee for Public Education and Religious Liberty v. Nyquist,
  413 U.S. 756 (1973)
Edwards v. Aguillard, 96 L.Ed.2d 510 or 482 U.S. ___ (1987)
Engel v. Vitale, 370 U.S. 421 (1962)
Epperson v. Arkansas, 393 U.S. 97 (1968)
Estate of Thornton v. Caldor, 472 U.S. 703 (1985)
Everson v. Board of Education, 330 U.S. 1 (1947)
Grand Rapids School District v. Ball, 473 U.S. 373 (1985)
Larkin v. Grendel's Den, 459 U.S. 116 (1982)
Larson v. Valente, 456 U.S. 228 (1982)
Latter Day Saints v. Amos, 483 U.S. 327 (1987)
Lemon v. Kurtzman, 403 U.S. 602 (1971)
Lynch v. Donnelly, 465 U.S. 668 (1984)
McCollum v. Board of Education, 333 U.S. 203 (1948)
McGowan v. Maryland, 366 U.S. 420 (1961)

Marsh v. Chambers, 463 U.S. 783 (1983)

Meek v. Pittenger, 421 U.S. 349 (1975)

Mueller v. Allen, 463 U.S. 388 (1983)

Roemer v. Board of Public Works of Maryland, 426 U.S. 736
 (1976)

Tilton v. Richardson, 403 U.S. 672 (1971)

Wallace v. Jaffre, 472 U.S. 38 (1985)

Walz v. Tax Commission of the City of New York, 397 U.S. 644
 (1970)

Witters v. Washington, 474 U.S. ___ (1986)

Wolman v. Walter, 433 U.S. 229 (1977)

Zorach v. Clauson, 343 U.S. 306 (1952)

CHAPTER I

1. *Providence Journal,* 22 December 1980.
2. Barbara Carton, "Pawtucket's Mayor Says, 'Bah, Humbug' to ACLU Grinches," *Providence Journal,* 20 December 1980, sec. A.
3. Sherbert v. Verner, 374 U.S. 398 (1963). Two recent exceptions to the Court's support for freedom of religion are U.S. v. Lee (1982), in which the Court ruled that the broad public interest in maintaining a sound social security system required that Amish citizens must pay social security taxes for their workers despite their religious objections; and Goldman v. Weinberger (1986), which sustained the right of the military to impose uniformity in dress regulations, thus preventing an Orthodox Jew from wearing his yarmulke indoors while in uniform.
4. Lemon v. Kurtzman, 403 U.S. 602 (1971) at 612.
5. Morris B. Abram, "Is Strict Separation Too Strict?" *Public Interest* 82 (Winter 1986): 82.
6. Citizens Concerned for Separation of Church and State v. Denver, 508 F. Supp. 382 (1980).
7. Florey v. Sioux Falls School District, 619 F. 2d. 131 (1980).
8. James Feron, "Larchmont Board Ends Creche Display," *New York Times,* 10 December 1975.
9. Joseph Berger, "December Dilemma for Non-Christians," *New York Times,* 10 December 1986, sec. B.
10. David R. Carlin, "Pawtucket and Its Nativity Scene," *Commonweal* 110 (16 December 1983).
11. Ibid.
12. Ibid.
13. Barbara Carton, "Nativity Scene Participants Speak Out," *Providence Journal,* 6 December 1981, sec. A.
14. Editorial, *Pawtucket Evening Times,* 18 December 1980.
15. John R. Khorey, "Nativity Scene Foe Finds He's Become a Pariah to Many," *Providence Journal,* 16 February 1981, and testimony at the district court trial on February 3, 1981.

16. "Letters to the Editor," *Pawtucket Evening Times,* 27 December 1980.

17. Ibid., 6 January 1981.

18. Ibid., 27 December 1980.

19. Carton, "Nativity Scene Participants Speak Out."

20. Editorial, *The Visitor* (Providence, R.I.), 1 January 1981.

21. *Civil Liberties in Depth,* American Civil Liberties Union Foundation of Rhode Island, 1, no. 5 (December 1982).

22. Background information on the ACLU is taken from *Guardian of Liberty,* a pamphlet published by the organization.

23. Edwards v. Aguillard, 96 L. Ed. 2d 510 or 482 U.S. ____ (1987).

24. Brown's statement was drafted by the author from a number of sources, including an interview with Brown on 21 September 1987 at ACLU offices in Providence. The printed record of Brown's position also includes interviews in the *Providence Journal* (11 January 1981) and the *Good News Paper* 1, no. 3 (January 1981). Portions of the statement were taken from the transcript of a debate between Brown and Mayor Lynch at the Roosevelt Center of American Policy Studies and from his testimony at the district court trial in Providence on 3–6 February 1981. Brown has read and approved the statement.

25. Mayor Lynch's statement was drafted by the author from a number of sources, including an interview on 21 September 1987 in the office of the state purchasing agent. The printed record of Lynch's position includes articles from the *Providence Journal* of 18–21 December 1980 and 7 February 1981. An interview in the *Good News Paper* 1, no. 3 (January 1981) and excerpts from the transcript of a debate between Mayor Lynch and Stephen Brown at the Roosevelt Center of American Policy Studies are also included, as is material from the trial in federal district court in Providence, 3–6 February 1981. Mayor Lynch has read and approved the statement.

26. Excerpts from witness testimony were selected from the version of the trial transcript appended to the Supreme Court records in Lynch v. Donnelly, 465 U.S. 668 (1984).

CHAPTER II

1. Stephen L. Wasby, *The Supreme Court in the Federal Judicial System,* 3d. ed. (Chicago: Nelson Hall, 1988), 45.

2. The few exceptions include appeals from territorial, bankruptcy, and other specialized courts.

3. In special situations, most often in cases arising from the Civil Rights

Act of 1964 and the Voting Rights Act of 1965, three-judge panels may sit.

4. Presidents are reluctant to challenge the practice of senatorial courtesy because custom in the Senate gives a member the right to "blackball" a federal judicial nomination to the district court in the senator's state.

5. The FBI conducts security and background checks on nominees. The ABA's Committee on the Federal Judiciary evaluates the legal competence of the nominees.

6. Charles Wyzanski, "The Importance of the Trial Judge," in *Courts, Judges, and Politics,* ed. Walter F. Murphy and C. Herman Pritchett (New York: Random House, 1974), 355.

7. Barbara Carton, "Nativity Scene Participants Speak Out," *Providence Journal,* 6 December 1981, sec. A.

8. Jeffrey T. Leeds, "A Life on the Court," *New York Times,* 5 October 1986, sec. IV.

9. In Gitlow v. New York, 282 U.S. 652 (1925), the Supreme Court used incorporation for the first time by applying freedom of speech in the First Amendment to the states.

10. Three pre-1947 cases that ruled on establishment are Bradford v. Roberts, 175 U.S. 1 (1899), Reuben Quick Bear v. Leupp, 210 U.S. 50 (1908), and Cochran v. Louisiana, 281 U.S. 370 (1930).

11. Everson v. Board of Education, 330 U.S. 1 (1947) at 15–16.

12. Idem, at 17–18.

13. Idem, at 44.

14. Norman Redlich, "The Separation of Church and State: The Burger Court's Tortuous Journey," in *The Burger Years: Rights and Wrongs in the Supreme Court,* ed. Herman Schwartz (New York: Penguin Books, 1988), 60.

15. McCollum v. Board of Education, 333 U.S. 203 (1948) at 210.

16. Idem, at 227.

17. Zorach v. Clauson, 343 U.S. 306 (1952) at 313–14.

18. McGowan v. Maryland, 366 U.S. 420 (1961), and Braunfield v. Brown, 366 U.S. 599 (1961).

19. Sherbert v. Verner, 347 U.S. 398 (1963).

20. Engel v. Vitale, 370 U.S. 421 (1962).

21. Abington Township v. Schempp, 374 U.S. 203 (1963) at 226.

22. Elder Witt, ed., *Guide to the U.S. Supreme Court* (Washington, D.C.: Congressional Quarterly Press, 1979), 495.

23. Walz v. Tax Commission, 397 U.S. 644 (1970) at 675.

24. Lemon v. Kurtzman, 403 U.S. 602 (1971) at 615.

25. Stone v. Graham, 449 U.S. 39 (1980) at 41.

26. Leonard W. Levy, *The Establishment Clause* (New York: Macmillan, 1986), 129.

27. Flast v. Cohen, 393 U.S. 83 (1968) at 111.

28. An amicus curiae brief is a document filed with the court by an individual or organization that is not directly involved in a suit but that has an interest in the result. Amicus briefs are discussed in more detail in Chapter IV.

29. U.S. District Court for the District of Rhode Island, *Plaintiff's Post-Trial Memorandum*, Donnelly v. Lynch, 525 F. Supp. 1150 (1981) at 12.

30. Robert A. Destro, *Brief of Amicus Curiae*, 16–17.

31. *Plaintiff's Post-Trial Memorandum, Donnelly v. Lynch* at 18.

32. U.S. District Court for the District of Rhode Island, *Defense's Post-Trial Memorandum, Donnelly v. Lynch* at 11.

33. Idem, at 12.

34. Idem, at 22.

35. *Plaintiff's Post-Trial Memorandum, Donnelly v. Lynch* at 24.

36. Idem, at 25.

37. *Defense's Post-Trial Memorandum, Donnelly v. Lynch* at 26–27.

38. Because of the length of Judge Pettine's opinion, it has been necessary to present it in edited form. For the full text, see *Donnelly v. Lynch.*

CHAPTER III

1. Barbara Carton, "Nativity Scene Participants Speak Out," *Providence Journal*, 6 December 1981, sec. A.

2. *Pawtucket Evening Times*, 10 November 1981.

3. *Pawtucket Evening Times*, 11 November 1981.

4. Editorial, *Pawtucket Evening Times*, 13 November 1981.

5. *Providence Journal*, 12 December 1981.

6. Editorial, *Pawtucket Evening Times*, 11 November 1981.

7. *Pawtucket Evening Times*, 19 November 1981.

8. Ibid.

9. Editorial, *Providence Journal*, 12 November 1981.

10. Carton, "Nativity Scene Participants Speak Out."

11. In addition to the twelve geographical circuits, the U.S. Court of Appeals for the Federal Circuit is a twelve-judge specialized appeals court hearing cases in patent, trademark, and copyright cases.

12. Stephen L. Wasby, *The Supreme Court in the Federal Judicial System*, 3d ed. (Chicago: Nelson Hall, 1988), 55.

13. Ibid., 47.

14. *Almanac of the Federal Judiciary*, vol. 2 (Chicago: Law Letters, 1987). The almanac surveys attorneys for their perceptions of the judges and their decisions.

15. Excerpts from the court of appeals opinion are taken from Donnelly v. Lynch 691 F2d 1029 (1982).

16. Wasby, *The Supreme Court*, 58.

17. Editorial, *Providence Journal*, 14 December 1982.

18. Karen Hupp, "Creche Course: Supreme Court," *Pawtucket Evening Times*, 8 November 1982.

CHAPTER IV

1. Loren P. Beth, *Politics, the Constitution, and the Supreme Court* (Evanston, Ill: Row, Peterson, and Co., 1962), 22–23.

2. Alexis de Tocqueville, *Democracy in America*, vol. 1 (New York: Vantage Books, 1954), 157.

3. William H. Rehnquist, *The Supreme Court: How It Was, How It Is* (New York: William Morrow and Co., 1988), 253.

4. For a more complete discussion of the Supreme Court's jurisdiction, see Henry J. Abraham, *The Judiciary*, 7th ed. (Boston: Allyn and Bacon, 1987), 25–32.

5. Rehnquist, *The Supreme Court*, 269.

6. Two four-week recesses occur between mid-December and March 1.

7. Rehnquist, *The Supreme Court*, 263–64.

8. The summary and the direct quotations are from *A Petition for a Writ of Certiorari to the United States Court of Appeals for the First Circuit*, which is part of the official record of Lynch v. Donnelly, 465 U.S. 668 (1984). Note that petitions for certiorari are filed with the Supreme Court through the court that last considered the case.

9. The summary and direct quotations are from *A Brief in Opposition to the Petition for a Writ of Certiorari to the United States Court of Appeals for the First Circuit*, which is part of the record in Lynch v. Donnelly, 465 U.S. 668 (1984).

10. Mueller v. Allen, 463 U.S. 388 (1983).

11. Marsh v. Chambers, 463 U.S. 783 (1983).

12. Editorial, *New York Times*, 19 September 1983, sec. A.

13. Quoted material in this section is taken from *Brief of the Petitioners* and *Reply Brief of the Petitioners*, which are part of the record of *Lynch v. Donnelly*.

14. *Brief for the United States as Amicus Curiae Supporting Reversal*, idem.

15. *Brief of Amicus Curiae for the Washington Legal Foundation; Brief of Amicus Curiae for the Legal . . . America; and Brief of Amicus Curiae for the Coalition of Religious Liberty and the Freedom Council,* idem.

16. *Brief of the Respondents,* idem.

17. *Brief of Amici Curiae of the Anti-Defamation League of B'nai B'rith and the American Jewish Committee in Support of the Respondents;* and *Brief of the American Jewish Committee and the National Council of Churches in the U.S.A. as Amici Curiae in Support of the Respondents,* idem.

18. Rehnquist, *The Supreme Court,* 276.

19. Alan F. Westin, *The Anatomy of a Constitutional Law Case* (New York: Macmillan, 1958), 129.

20. Stephen L. Wasby, *The Supreme Court in the Federal Judicial System,* 3d ed. (Chicago: Nelson Hall, 1988), 116.

21. David Danelski, "The Influence of the Chief Justice in the Decisional Process," in *Courts, Judges, and Politics,* ed. Walter F. Murphy and C. Herman Pritchett (New York: Random House, 1961), 497–508.

22. Rehnquist, *The Supreme Court,* 290.

23. Ibid., 296.

24. Ibid., 302.

25. Eugene V. Rostow, "The Democratic Character of Judicial Review," *Harvard Law Review* 66 (December 1952): 208.

26. Because the decision was extraordinarily lengthy, an edited version is included here. The full text of the opinion is located in *Lynch* v. *Donnelly.*

CHAPTER V

1. Lynch v. Donnelly, 465 U.S. 668 (1984) at 264.

2. Idem, at 645.

3. *Woonsocket Call,* cited in "The Pawtucket Creche Case: The Supreme Court Rules," *Civil Liberties in Depth,* American Civil Liberties Union of Rhode Island No. 7 (April 1984).

4. Editorial, *Pawtucket Evening Times,* 8 March 1984.

5. Editorial in *Barrington Times,* cited in "The Pawtucket Creche Case."

6. James Kaull, "A Victory Christians Don't Need," *Providence Journal,* 8 March 1984, sec. A.

7. Lynch's statement is in the form of a letter to the author dated 8 February 1988.

8. Dudley Clendinen, "Ruling on Christmas Display Elates People in Pawtucket," *New York Times,* 6 March 1984, sec. B.

9. Stephen Brown's statement is in the form of a letter to the author dated 30 January 1988.

10. John Kifney, "Bishop Gelineau Agrees City Hall Improper Spot for Nativity Scene," *Providence Journal,* 18 December 1984, sec. A.

11. Barbara Polichetti, "Barrington Citizens' Group Votes to Defy the Council," *Providence Journal,* 18 December 1984, sec. A.

12. Judge Pettine's remarks are taken from accounts in the *Providence Journal* on 27 October 1984, sec. A, and 2 November 1984, sec. A. Judge Pettine reviewed and approved the statement.

13. George Will, "Wise Men and Pawtucket," *Washington Post,* 11 March 1984, sec. C.

14. Ibid.

15. James J. Kilpatrick, "A U.S. Creche? No," *Washington Post,* 30 November 1984, sec. A.

16. Editorial, *Wall Street Journal,* 7 March 1984.

17. Quoted in "The Pawtucket Creche Case."

18. Ibid.

19. Ibid.

20. Editorial, *New York Times,* 8 March 1984 sec. A.

21. Meg Greenfield, "The Grinches vs. the Creche," *Newsweek,* 24 December 1985, p. 72.

22. Karen Hupp, "They Lost the Case, but Continue the Fight," *Pawtucket Evening Times,* 6 March 1984.

23. Linda Greenhouse, "High Court Rules City May Put Up Nativity Display," *New York Times,* 6 March 1984, sec. I.

24. Ibid.

25. Ibid.

26. Norman Redlich, "Nativity Ruling Insults Jews," *New York Times,* 26 March 1984, sec. A.

27. A complete list of the articles is included in the bibliography.

28. Glenn S. Gordon, "*Lynch* v. *Donnelly:* Breaking Down the Barriers to Religious Displays," *Cornell Law Review* 71 (November 1985): 188.

29. Jacqueline M. Gerber, "*Lynch* v. *Donnelly:* One Foot off the Tightrope," *Northern Illinois University Law Review* 5 (Winter 1984): 125.

30. Kenneth M. Cox, "The Lemon Test Soured," *Vanderbilt Law Review* 37 (October 1984): 1179.

31. "The Supreme Court, 1983 Term," *Harvard Law Review* 98 (November 1984): 177–84.

32. Joshua D. Zarrow, "Of Crosses and Creches," *American University Law Review* 35 (Winter 1986): 506.

33. Gerber, "*Lynch* v. *Donnelly,*" 144.

34. David C. Fairchild, "*Lynch v. Donnelly:* The Case for the Creche," *St. Louis University Law Journal* 29 (March 1985): 485.

35. Ibid.

36. Yehudah Mirsky, "Civil Religion and the Establishment Clause," *Yale Law Journal* 95 (May 1986): 1246.

37. Cox, "Lemon Test," passim.

38. McCreary v. Stone, 575 F. Supp. 1112 (1983).

39. McCreary v. Stone, 739 F. 2d. 716 (1984).

40. Board of Trustees v. McCreary, 105 S. Ct. 1959 (1985).

41. ACLU v. City of Birmingham, 588 F. Supp. 1337 (1984).

42. ACLU v. City of Birmingham, 791 F. 2d. 1561 (1986).

43. American Jewish Congress v. City of Chicago, 827 F. 2d. 120 (1987).

44. ACLU v. Allegheny County, 842 F. 2d. 655 (1988) at 662.

45. On 3 July 1989, the Court ruled, 5–4, that the display of the creche was unconstitutional. However, by a 6–3 vote the Court upheld the right of the city to display the menorah. Speaking for a different majority in each part of the case, Justice Blackmun, aligned with Justice O'Connor on both questions, ruled that the creche, unaccompanied by secular symbols of the holiday season, gave the impression that the county was endorsing the religious message of the display. The menorah, situated next to a Christmas tree and a sign saluting liberty, is "not an endorsement of religious faith but simply a recognition of cultural diversity."

Context was the key for the two swing justices. O'Connor wrote a concurring opinion in which she argued for "the appearance of religious endorsement" test she spoke to in *Lynch*. Brennan, Marshall, and Stevens joined the majority in the creche opinion but dissented on the menorah. The newest member of the Court, Anthony Kennedy, concurred with the majority on the issue of the menorah but wrote a dissenting opinion on the creche part of the decision that was joined by Justices Rehnquist, White, and Scalia.

46. Eugene Sand and Gravel v. City of Eugene, 276 Or 1007 (1978).

47. Greater Houston Chapter of ACLU v. Eckels, 589 F. Supp. 222 (1984).

48. James Brooke, "Crosses Dot Greenwich in Protest of Ban by Judge," *New York Times,* 25 December 1985, sec. I.

49. "Judge in Mississippi Bans Cross Display on State Building," *New York Times,* 13 December 1986.

50. ACLU v. City of St. Charles, 794 F. 2d. 265 (1986) at 273.

51. Walz v. Tax Commission, 397 U.S. 664 (1970) at 672.

52. Gerber, "*Lynch v. Donnelly*," 123.

CHAPTER VI

1. Mark DeWolfe Howe, *The Garden and the Wilderness: Religion and the Government in American Constitutional History* (Chicago: University of Chicago Press, 1965), 4.

2. See for example, Michael Perry, *The Constitution, the Courts, and Human Rights* (New Haven: Yale University Press, 1982), and Richard E. Morgan, *Disabling America: The "Rights Industry" in Our Time* (New York: Basic Books, 1984).

3. See William J. Brennan, Jr., "The Constitution of the United States: Contemporary Ratification," speech delivered at Text and Teaching Symposium, Georgetown University, Washington, D.C., 12 October 1985.

4. Lynch v. Donnelly, 465 U.S. 668 (1984) at 673.

5. Brennan, "The Constitution," 5.

6. Morgan, *Disabling America,* 16.

7. Robert L. Cord, *Separation of Church and State, Historical Fact and Current Fiction* (New York: Lambeth, 1982), 110.

8. Morgan, *Disabling America,* 13.

9. See Cord, *Separation,* chaps. 2 and 5, which critique the separationist positions and in particular the work of Leo Pfeffer.

10. Ibid., 213.

11. Wallace v. Jaffre, 472 U.S. 38 (1985) at 110.

12. The best and most recent discussion of how separationist scholars view the original intentions of the Framers of the Establishment Clause is Leonard W. Levy's *The Establishment Clause* (New York: Macmillan, 1986).

13. Ibid., 84.

14. Ibid., xiii.

15. Marsh v. Chambers, 463 U.S. 783 (1983) at 817.

16. *Lynch v. Donnelly* at 718.

17. Idem.

18. Richard H. Jones, "Accommodationist and Separationist Ideals in Supreme Court Establishment Decisions," *Journal of Church and State* 28 (Spring 1986): 223.

19. Laurence Parisot, "Attitudes About the Media: A Five Country Comparison," *Public Opinion* 10 (January–February 1988): 19.

20. Zorach v. Clauson, 343 U.S. 306 (1952) at 313.

21. *Lynch v. Donnelly* at 696.

22. Morris B. Abram, "Is Strict Separation Too Strict?" *Public Interest* 82 (Winter 1986): 90.

23. Philip Johnson, "Concept and Compromise: First Amendment Religious Doctrine," *California Law Review* (September 1984): 839–40.

24. Laurence Tribe, *American Constitutional Law* (Mineola, N.Y.: Founders Press, 1978), 834.

25. Ibid., 819.

26. Abington Township v. Schempp, 374 U.S. 203 (1963) at 281.

27. Widmar v. Vincent, 454 U.S. 263 (1981) at 267, 271.

28. *Wallace v. Jaffre* at 106.

29. Everson v. Board of Education, 330 U.S. 1 (1947) at 24.

30. Board of Education v. Allen, 392 U.S. 236 (1968) at 250.

31. *Everson v. Board of Education* at 32.

32. *Marsh v. Chambers* at 822.

33. Idem.

34. Brennan, "The Constitution," 10.

35. Cited in Walter F. Murphy et al., *Courts, Judges, and Politics,* 2d ed. (New York: Random House, 1974), 11.

36. Ibid., 27.

BIBLIOGRAPHY

BOOKS

Abraham, Henry J. *The Judiciary.* 7th ed. Boston: Allyn and Bacon, 1987.

Almanac of the Federal Judiciary. 2 vols. Chicago: Law Letters, 1988.

Beth, Loren P. *Politics, the Constitution, and the Supreme Court.* Evanston, Ill.: Row, Peterson, and Co., 1962.

Commanger, Henry Steele. *Freedom of Religion and Separation of Church and State.* Mount Vernon, N.Y.: A. Colish, 1985.

Cord, Robert L. *Separation of Church and State: Historical Fact and Current Fiction.* New York: Lambeth, 1982.

Howe, Mark DeWolfe. *The Garden and the Wilderness: Religion and the Government in American Constitutional History.* Chicago: University of Chicago Press, 1965.

Lee, Francis G. *Wall of Controversy: Church–State Conflict in America.* Malabar, Fla.: Krieger, 1986.

Levy, Leonard W. *The Establishment Clause.* New York: Macmillan, 1986.

Malbin, Michael J. *Religion and Politics: The Intentions of the Authors of the First Amendment.* Washington, D.C.: American Enterprise Institute, 1978.

Miller, Robert T., and Ronald B. Flowers. *Toward Benevolent Neutrality: Church, State and the Supreme Court.* 3d ed. Waco, Tex.: Baylor University Press, 1987.

Morgan, Richard E. *Disabling America: The "Rights Industry" in Our Time.* New York: Basic Books, 1984.

Murphy, Walter F. et al., eds. *Courts, Judges, and Politics.* 2d ed. New York: Random House, 1974.

Perry, Michael. *The Constitution, The Courts, and Human Rights.* New Haven: Yale University Press, 1982.

Pfeffer, Leo. *Church, State and Freedom.* Revised and enlarged ed. Boston: Beacon Press, 1967.

Rehnquist, William H. *The Supreme Court: How It Was, How It Is.* New York: William Morrow and Co., 1988.

Schwartz, Herman, ed. *The Burger Years: Rights and Wrongs in the Supreme Court.* New York: Penguin Books, 1988.

Tocqueville, Alexis de. *Democracy in America.* Vol. 1. New York: Vantage Books, 1954.

Tribe, Laurence. *American Constitutional Law.* Mineola, N.Y.: Founders Press, 1978.

Wasby, Stephen L. *The Supreme Court in the Federal Judicial System.* 3d ed. Chicago: Nelson Hall, 1988.

Westin, Alan F. *The Anatomy of a Constitutional Law Case.* New York: Macmillan, 1958.

Witt, Elder, ed. *Guide to the United States Supreme Court.* Washington, D.C.: Congressional Quarterly Press, 1979.

JOURNAL ARTICLES

Abram, Morris B. "Is Strict Separation Too Strict?" *Public Interest* 82 (Winter 1986): 81–90.

Best, James. "The Rebirth of the Supreme Court's Attitude Toward the Establishment Clause." *Southern University Law Review* 12 (Fall 1985): 97–105.

Boatti, Robert. "*Lynch v. Donnelly,*" *Rutgers Law Review* 37 (Fall 1984): 103–36.

Brennan, Shauna, et al. "Establishment Clause Scrutiny of Nativity Scene Displays." *Notre Dame Law Review* 62 (December 1986): 114–24.

Camras, Barbara J. "A New Interpretation of the Establishment Clause." *University of West Los Angeles Law Review* 17 (1985): 101–25.

Carlin, David R. "Pawtucket and Its Nativity Scene," *Commonweal* 110 (16 December 1983): 682–83.

"Confusion in the Court." *America* 152 (22 June 1985): 501.

Cox, Kenneth M. "The Lemon Test Soured." *Vanderbilt Law Review* 37 (October 1984): 1175–203.

Crabb, Kelly C. "Religious Symbols, American Traditions, and the Constitution." *Brigham Young Law Review* (February 1984): 509–62.

Devins, Neal. "Aftermath of the *Lynch* Decision: Raising New Constitutional Issues." *National Law Journal* (16 April 1984): 18, 20.

———. "Religious Symbols and the Establishment Clause." *Journal of Church and State* 27 (Winter 1985): 19–46.

Dorsen, Norman, and Charles Sims. "The Nativity Scene Case: An Error of Judgement." *University of Illinois Law Review* (Fall 1985): 837–68.

Drinan, Robert F. "Is a Christmas Creche Legal in 1986?" *America* 155 (13 December 1986): 375.

———. "The Supreme Court, Religious Freedom and the Yarmulke." *America* 155 (12 July 1986): 9–11.

———. "The Supreme Court and Scarsdale's Creche." *America* 153 (8 December 1984): 377.

Fairchild, David C. "*Lynch v. Donnelly:* The Case for the Creche." *St. Louis University Law Journal* 29 (March 1985): 459–88.

Ford, Maurice deG. "Creche Landing," *Commonweal* 111 (6 April 1984): 202–3.

"From Poland to Pawtucket." Editorial. *Commonweal* 111 (6 April 1984): 196.

Fuchs, Jill N. "Publicly Funded Displays of Religious Symbols." *University of Cincinnati Law Review* 51 (Spring 1982): 353–72.

Garvey, John. "That Old Civil Religion." *Commonweal* 110 (4 November 1983): 583–84.

Gerber, Jacqueline M. "*Lynch* v. *Donnelly:* One Foot off the Tightrope." *Northern Illinois University Law Review* 5 (Winter 1984): 123–54.

Gibson, John B. "A Christian Christmas in Pawtucket." *Washburn Law Journal* 24 (Fall 1984): 135–51.

Gordon, Glenn S. "*Lynch* v. *Donnelly:* Breaking Down the Barriers to Religious Displays." *Cornell Law Review* 71 (November 1985): 185–208.

Grant, Harriet. "The Disappearing Wall." *North Carolina Law Review* 63 (April 1985): 782–93.

Greenfield, Meg. "The Grinches vs. The Creche." *Newsweek* 104 (24 December 1985): 72.

Johnson, Philip. "Concept and Compromise: First Amendment Religious Doctrine." *California Law Review* (September 1984): 817–46.

Jones, Richard H. "Accommodationist and Separationist Ideals in Supreme Court Establishment Clause Decisions." *Journal of Church and State* 28 (Spring 1986): 192–223.

Katz, Naomi. "One Giant Step over the Wall." *Pace University Law Review* 5 (Fall 1984): 81–109.

Kaufman, Irving R. "What Did the Founding Fathers Intend?" *New York Times Magazine* (23 February 1988): 42.

Long, Patricia D. "Does the Wall Still Stand?" *Baylor Law Review* 37 (Summer 1975): 755–75.

Middleton, Martha. "City Hall Creche Unconstitutional." *National Law Journal* (7 September 1987).

Mirsky, Yehudah. "Civil Religion and the Establishment Clause." *Yale Law Journal* 95 (May 1986): 1237–57.

"Nativity and Sensitivity." Editorial. *Commonweal* 112 (29 November 1985): 659.

Parisot, Laurence. "Attitudes About the Media: A Five Country Comparison." *Public Opinion* 10 (January–February 1988): 18–20.

"The Pawtucket Creche Case: The Supreme Court Rules." *Civil Liberties in Depth* 7 (April 1984): 1–8.

Rogers, Sidney M. "*Lynch* v. *Donnelly:* Our Christmas Will Be Merry Still." *Mercer Law Review* 36 (Fall 1984): 409–20.

Rostow, Eugene V. "The Democratic Character of Judicial Review." *Harvard Law Review* 66 (December 1952): 193–224.

Selle, Elaine. "Christ in Christmas." *Loyola University Law Review* 30 (Fall 1984): 1059–74.

Simon, Harry. "Rebuilding the Wall Between Church and State." *Hastings Law Journal* (June 1986): 499–534.

Stewart, David O. "Taking Christ out of Christmas?" *American Bar Association Journal* 69 (December 1983): 1832–37.

"The Supreme Court, 1983 Term." *Harvard Law Review* 98 (November 1984): 174–84.

Sutton, Wendell Blair. "Constitutional Law: *Lynch* v. *Donnelly.*" *Oklahoma Law Review* 38 (Fall 1985): 535–62.

TRB. "Away with a Manger." *New Republic* 193 (31 October 1983): 4.

Van Alstyne, William. "Mr. Jefferson's Crumbling Wall." *Duke Law Journal* (Summer 1984): 770–87.

Weiss, Abraham. "The Menorah–Creche Controversy." *New York Law Journal* 192 (26 December 1984): 2.

Zarrow, Joshua D. "Of Crosses and Creches." *American University Law Review* 35 (Winter 1986): 477–516.

NEWSPAPER ARTICLES

"ACLU v. Christmas." Editorial. *Pawtucket Evening Times.* 11 November 1981.

Barbash, Fred. "City-Funded Creche Is Permitted." *Washington Post,* 6 March 1984, sec. A.

———. "Justices Consider Santa Clauses, Colored Lights, and Creches." *Washington Post,* 5 October 1983, sec. A.

———. "Right to Display Creche Backed by Justice Department." *Washington Post,* 1 July 1983, sec. A.

Berger, Joseph. "December Dilemma for Non-Christians." *New York Times,* 10 December 1986, sec. B.

Brooke, James. "Crosses Dot Greenwich in Protest of Ban by Judge." *New York Times,* 25 December 1985, sec. I.

Brown, Thomas S. "Pawtucket Officials Elated at Court 'Triumph.'" *Providence Journal*, 6 March 1984, sec. A.

———. "Shoppers Enjoy Christmas Display." *Providence Journal*, 4 December 1981, sec. A.

Carmel, Jeffrey J. "Pawtucket's Creche Shifts to Private Park." *Christian Science Monitor*, 20 October 1983.

Carton, Barbara. "Lynch Espies 'Scrooge' Under Tree," *Providence Journal*, 19 December 1981.

———. "Nativity Scene Participants Speak Out." *Providence Journal*, 6 December 1981.

———. "Pawtucket's Mayor Says, 'Bah, Humbug' to ACLU Grinches." *Providence Journal*, 21 December 1980.

"Church/State: Judge Pettine Speaks Out." Editorial, *Providence Journal*, 2 November 1984, sec. A.

"City Halls and Christmas: A Constitutional View." Editorial, *Providence Journal*, 12 November 1981.

Clendinen, Dudley. "Ruling on Christmas Display Elates People in Pawtucket." *New York Times*, 6 March 1984, sec. B.

———. "For Supreme Court's Calendar, a Rhode Island Nativity Scene." *New York Times*, 18 December 1983.

Cohen, Richard. "Creche Course." *Washington Post*, October 6 1983, sec. B.

Dujardin, Richard C. "Religious Leaders Divided on Display of Nativity Scenes." *Providence Journal*, 7 December 1983, sec. A.

———. "State Religious Leaders Mostly Dismayed by Decision." *Providence Journal*, 6 March 1984, sec. A.

Ellsworth, Karen. "ACLU Files Lawsuit Against Pawtucket's Christmas Display." *Providence Journal*, 18 December 1980.

———. "Nativity Scene Suits Revive Church–State Controversy." *Providence Evening Bulletin*, 23 December 1981.

———. "Pettine Delays Ruling on Nativity Display." *Providence Journal*, 20 December 1980.

Feron, James. "Creche Put Up in Scarsdale." *New York Times*, 20 December 1985, sec. I.

———. "Larchmont Board Ends Creche Display." *New York Times*, 10 December 1975.

———. "Suit Challenges Scarsdale Creche Ban." *New York Times*, 21 July 1983, sec. B.

Garreau, Joel. "Of a Town That Took a Nativity Scene to the Supreme Court." *Washington Post*, 25 December 1983, Sec. B.

Gaulin, Ed. "Lynch Urges Nativity Appeal." *Pawtucket Evening Times,* 13 November 1981.

Goldman, Ari L. "Reaction Is Mixed on Nativity Ruling." *New York Times,* 6 March 1984, sec. I.

Greenhouse, Linda. "High Court Rules City May Put Up Nativity Display." *New York Times,* 6 March 1984, sec. I.

————. "New Issue Involving Nativity Scene." *New York Times,* 16 October 1984, sec. I.

————. "Scarsdale's Creche Ban Defended Before Justices." *New York Times,* 21 February 1985, sec. I.

Hupp, Karen. "Creche Course: Supreme Court." *Pawtucket Evening Times* 8 November 1982.

————. "They Lost the Case, but Continue the Fight." *Pawtucket Evening Times,* 6 March 1984.

"It's a Matter of Principle? You're Kidding." Editorial, *Pawtucket Evening Times,* 11 December 1980.

"Judge in Mississippi Bans Cross Display on State Building." *New York Times,* 13 December 1986.

Kaull, James. "A 'Victory' Christians Don't Need." *Providence Journal,* 8 March 1984, sec. A.

Khorey, John R. "Nativity Scene Foe Finds He's Become a Pariah to Many." *Providence Journal,* 16 February 1981.

Kifney, John. "Bishop Gelineau Agrees City Hall Improper Spot for Nativity Scene." *Providence Journal,* 18 December 1984, sec. A.

Kilpatrick, James J. "Creche and State." *Washington Post,* 7 October 1983, sec. A.

————. "A U.S. Creche? No." *Washington Post,* 30 November 1984, sec. A.

Kriza, Gregg. "Pettine Criticizes High Court Ruling on Nativity Scene." *Providence Journal,* 27 October 1984, sec. A.

Kur, Carol. "Jews at Christmas." *New York Times,* 24 December 1984, sec. I.

Leeds, Jeffrey T. "A Life on the Court." *New York Times,* 5 October 1986, sec. IV.

Levin, Rob. "Donahue, Nativity Scene Elicit Dual Passions." *Providence Journal,* 21 October 1983, sec. A.

Marot, David. "The Nativity Scene Debate." *Good News Paper* 1, no. 3 (January 1981).

Morgan, Thomas J. "Bishop Hunt Cautions Against Using Religion to Alter Public Policy." *Providence Journal,* 28 November 1984, sec. A.

————. "Clergymen Endorse ACLU Suit." *Providence Journal,* 23 December 1980.

Mulligan, John E. "Creche Ruled Constitutional as Secular 'Folk' Display." *Providence Journal,* 6 March 1984, sec. A.

"Nativity Scene: Appeal Decision." Editorial, *Pawtucket Evening Times,* 13 November 1981.

"Nativity Scene: Legal Issue Goes to Supreme Court." *Providence Journal,* 20 April 1983, sec. A.

Norman, Michael. "Our Towns." *New York Times,* 20 December 1984, sec. I.

"Permissible, if Slightly Profane." Editorial, *New York Times,* 8 March 1984, sec. I.

Polichetti, Barbara. "Barrington Citizens' Group Vows to Defy the Council." *Providence Journal,* 18 December 1984, sec. A.

Redlich, Norman. "Nativity Ruling Insults Jews." *New York Times,* 26 March 1984, sec. A.

Roberts, Greg. "It's Mayor Lynch Who Harms Religion, ACLU Head Asserts." *Providence Journal,* 11 January 1981.

"Sorting Out Symbols at Christmas Time." Editorial, *Providence Journal,* 14 December 1982, sec. A.

"Trivial Pursuits." Editorial, *Wall Street Journal,* 7 March 1984.

Turner, Darrell. "The Christmas Debate Continues." *Church World,* 11 December 1980.

"U.S. High Court Deadlocks on Scarsdale Creche Case." *New York Times.* 28 March 1985, sec. B.

"We Congratulate Mayor Lynch." Editorial, *The Visitor* (official newspaper of the Catholic diocese of Providence), 1 January 1981.

Will, George F. "Wise Men and Pawtucket." *Washington Post,* 11 March 1984, sec. C.